# On Dreams an

# On
# Dreams and Death

## A JUNGIAN INTERPRETATION

Marie-Louise von Franz

TRANSLATED BY
Emmanuel Xipolitas Kennedy
and Vernon Brooks

SHAMBHALA
Boston & London
1987

Shambhala Publications, Inc.
314 Dartmouth Street
Boston, Massachusetts 02116

© 1984 Kösel-Verlag GmbH & Co., Munich
Translation © 1986 Shambhala Publications, Inc.

9  8  7  6  5  4  3  2  1

First paperback edition

Printed in the United States of America
Distributed in the United States by Random House
and in Canada by Random House of Canada Ltd.


The Library of Congress Catalogues the hardback edition of
this work as follows:

Franz, Marie-Louise von, 1915–
    On dreams and death.

    Translation of: Traum und Tod.
    Bibliography: p.
    Includes index.
    1. Dreams   2. Death.   I. Title.
BF1099.D4F73   1986     155.9'37     85-27902
ISBN 0-87773-357-0
        0-394-55249-0 (Random House)
        0-87773-405-4 (pbk)


Thanks are extended to the following publishers and
institutions for permission to reprint material copy-
righted or controlled by them: The C. G. Jung Foundation for permission to quote from *Ego and Archetype* by
Edward Edinger, published by Putnam's Sons, New
York, for the C. G. Jung Foundation, New York, ©
1972; Pantheon Books, a division of Random House,
for permission to quote from *Memories, Dreams, Reflections* by C. G. Jung, recorded and edited by Aniela
Jaffe, translated by Richard and Clara Winston, ©
1961, 1962, 1963 by Random House, Inc.; and Princeton University Press for permission to quote from *Letters, Volume I: 1906–1950* of C. G. Jung, edited by
Gerhard Adler and Aniela Jaffe, translated by R.F.C.
Hull, Bollingen series XCV, © 1971, 1973 by Princeton University Press, and from *Letters, Volume II: 1951–
1961*, © 1953, 1975 by Princeton University Press.

# Contents

# Introduction

*U*nlike most contemporary publications on the subject of death, this study is not concerned with problems arising in the *treatment* of dying people. Instead, it deals primarily with what the unconscious of man, the world of his instincts and his dreams, has to say about the *fact* of impending death. As is generally known, we cannot manipulate dreams; they are, as it were, the voice of nature within us. They show us therefore the manner in which nature, through dreams, prepares us for death. This approach inevitably raises questions concerning the correct interpretation of the images in which dreams express themselves. Since we will be concerned with universal human structures, I have made special use of ethnological and alchemical material for the amplification of these structures and in order to consider the dreams within their more general context. Moreover, the alchemical tradition contains much more material on the problem of death than we find, for instance, in official religious traditions.

This work is therefore based, for the most part, on four general themes: (1) current-day death experiences and death dreams; (2) the basic concepts of Jungian psychology which apply to the second half of life and to death; (3) the death and resurrection symbolism of the Western alchemical tradition. It is with these three subjects that I feel most at home. I will also discuss briefly (4) certain aspects of parapsychological research.

One might ask—and with good reason, of course—whether another publication need be added to today's flood of literature on the subject of death.[1] Unfortunately, however, only a very few of the current works take dream manifestations of the unconscious into consideration or even mention them in passing. Elizabeth Kübler-Ross,[2] who for the most part deals with the development of the personality in the face of death, describes primarily those processes of consciousness which are externally observable and can be articulated. Events which take place in the depths of the unconscious, however, are still seldom investigated today. It is true that Edgar Herzog's *Psyche and Death* and Ingeborg Clarus' *Du stirbst, damit du lebst* deal with the subject of death from the point of view of C. G. Jung's psychology, but both works focus primarily on the "die and become" process as it occurs in the course of the individuation process during every lifetime, not on the dreams of individuals who happen to be near the end of their lives. As an exception, Barbara Hannah deals with the latter in her essay, "Regression oder Erneuerung im Alter" (Regression or Renewal in Old Age); and Edward Edinger in *Ego and Archetype* describes an impressive series of twelve dreams from a dying patient and provides an excellent interpretation of them. The inescapable relationship of the images in these dreams to images prevalent in the alchemical tradition is identified and emphasized. The valuable work of Jane Wheelwright in *Death of a Woman* should also be mentioned, for this volume describes the entire course of the analysis of a dying young woman.

References to dreams are also to be found occasionally in Mark Pelgrin's *And a Time to Die* and in Millie Kelly Fortier's *Dreams and Preparation for Death*, to which I will often refer. Moreover, David Eldred, in his dissertation, *The Psychodynamics of the Dying Process*, has collected and superbly analyzed the pictures painted by a simple Swiss woman dying of cancer. Almost all of the motifs which will be discussed in the present work appear in those pictures, for it looks as if certain basic archetypal structures exist in the depths of the soul which almost regularly come to the fore during the processes of dying. I will refer frequently to this work of Eldred.

To some extent I will also compare dream motifs with momentary "near-death experiences," as such experiences are described in the extensive current literature on death. The subject matter and its expression may not differ essentially from the imagery of the death experiences, but the dreams are far more subtle and richer in imagery. Compared to dreams, near-death experiences appear schematic and more specifically culture-formed. It seems to me that the individuals actually experience something inexpressible in the death experiences, which they then elaborate in culture-specific images. The dreams are in themselves more graphic and detailed.

The analysis of older people provides a wealth of dream symbols that psychically prepare the dreamers for impending death. It is in fact true, as Jung has emphasized, that the unconscious psyche pays very little attention to the abrupt end of bodily life and behaves as if the psychic life of the individual, that is, the individuation process, will simply continue. In this connection, however, there are also dreams which symbolically indicate the end of bodily life and the explicit continuation of psychic life after death. The unconscious "believes" quite obviously in a life after death.

The skeptic will naturally insist that these are merely wish-fulfillment dreams. One can say in reply that the theory that dreams reflect only unconscious wishes[3] does not accord at all with general experience. On the contrary, as Jung has shown, dreams more often depict a completely objective psychic "natural event," uninfluenced by the wishes of the ego. In cases where the dreamer has illusions about his approaching death or is unaware of its closeness, dreams may even indicate this fact quite brutally and mercilessly, as, for instance, in the motif of the dreamer's clock which has stopped and cannot be started again, or the theme of the life-tree, which has been hewn down and is lying on the ground.

Sometimes death is indicated even more explicitly. A colleague of mine kept company with a young woman whose entire body had been invaded by cancer. In the end the brain was infected, so that she was unconscious most of the time. The analyst continued to visit her, however, sitting quietly by her bedside. Twenty-four hours before she died, the patient suddenly opened her eyes and said that she had dreamed the following dream:

> I am standing beside my bed in the hospital room and I feel strong and healthy. Sunshine flows in through the window. The doctor is there and says, "Well, Miss X, you are unexpectedly completely cured. You may get dressed and leave the hospital." At that moment I turn around and see, lying in the bed—my own dead body!

The comforting message of the unconscious—that death is a "cure" and that there is an afterlife—obviously cannot be interpreted here as a wish-fulfillment dream, for at the same time the end of physical existence is also predicted, quite brutally and unequivocally.

In the course of this study, further dreams will be cited in which the end of bodily life is clearly depicted but which simultaneously always also contain statements—as in the above dream —that point to an afterlife. In this connection, Jung stresses that it is of great importance for the aging person to acquaint himself with the possibility of death.

> A categorical question is being put to him, and he is under an obligation to answer it. To this end he ought to have a myth about death, for reason shows him nothing but the dark pit into which he is descending. Myth, however, can conjure up other images for him, helpful and enriching pictures of life in the land of the dead. If he believes in them, or greets them with some measure of credence, he is being just as right or just as wrong as someone who does not believe in them. But while the man who despairs marches toward nothingness, the one who has placed his faith in the archetype follows the tracks of life and lives right into his death. Both, to be sure, remain in uncertainty, but the one lives against his instincts, the other with them.[4]

In the following material I will comment on archetypal death dreams and amplify them, for the most part through the symbolism of the Egyptian death ritual and through related alchemical symbolism—for a striking gap prevails in the official collective Christian concept of survival after death. It is true that Christianity teaches the immortality of the soul and the resurrection of the body; but the latter is supposed to occur abruptly at the end of the world through an act of God's grace in which the old body is somehow reproduced. This is a mystery which one must "believe." There are no indications of exactly "how" the miracle will occur.

In their zeal to present Christianity as something quite new and something preferable to other contemporary religions, most theologians[5] attempt to emphasize the *concrete* historical aspect, not only of the life of Jesus but also of his resurrection. They deny all connection with such dying and resurrecting nature gods of antiquity as Attis, Adonis, Osiris, and criticize the pagan religions for lack of clarity, for uncertainty, and the like. Friedrich Nötscher, for instance, stresses the vagueness of Egyptian Near Eastern after-death ideas and devaluates many Old Testament concepts, even reducing them to mere figures of speech.[6] Such an attitude results in great *symbol impoverishment*. The non-Biblical religions of late antiquity may admittedly contain vaguenesses and apparent contradictions; nevertheless, they have the merit of conveying a rich symbolic world of representations regarding death, resurrection and postmortal life—archetypal images that the soul of contemporary man also produces quite spontaneously today. There is, moreover, another difference between such spontaneous products of the unconscious and official Christian teaching. In the latter man remains completely passive vis-à-vis the event of resurrection; a pure act of God's grace returns his body to him. In the alchemical tradition, on the other hand, the adept in the alchemical work, the *opus* (which admittedly can only succeed through God's grace), creates his own resurrected body during his lifetime. Certain Eastern methods of meditation are also supposed to assist in creating a "diamond body," which survives physical death.

Today, however, many contemporary theologians of both Christian confessions have broken away from the concretistic views of early Christian times. For them, resurrection has become an "immanent anticipation"; that is, since linear, historical time stops with death, the "Judgment" or the "Final Judgment" (according to Boros) can be understood as taking place just after death.[7] Or, as Karl Rahner expresses it, after his death man becomes "all-cosmic" and passes into the concrete ontological *materia prima* of the universe, where he encounters Christ as "Lord of the World."[8] Resurrection is in these views no longer considered to be a recreation of the old body but is seen as a prolonged existence of the subject in a spiritual body or a kind of "internalized matter."[9] Such a process of the interiorization of matter or of the world background is easily postulated. Contrary to this, the ancient alchemists actually attempted again and again to penetrate *empirically* into the secret of life after death, creating mythical symbols which strikingly resemble the dreams—spontaneous unconscious products—of modern people.

In his introduction to *Psychology and Alchemy*, Jung describes how the development of motifs in alchemical symbolism compensates for the overly one-sided spiritual orientation of Christianity:

> Alchemy is rather like an undercurrent to the Christianity that ruled on the surface. It is to this surface as the dream is to consciousness, and just as the dream compensates the conflicts of the conscious mind, so alchemy endeavours to fill in the gaps left by the Christian tension of opposites. . . . The historical shift in the world's consciousness towards the masculine is compensated by the chthonic femininity of the unconscious. In certain pre-Christian religions the male principle had already been differentiated in the father-son specification, a change which was to be of the utmost importance for Christianity. Were the unconscious merely complementary, this change of consciousness would have been accompanied by the production of a mother and daughter, for which the necessary material lay ready to hand in the myth of Demeter and Persephone. But, as alchemy shows, the unconscious chose rather the Cybele-Attis type in the form of the *prima materia* and the *filius macrocosmi*, thus proving that it is not complementary but compensatory.[10]

Our present uncertainty concerning death is a place where this process of compensation also tends to occur; for Christianity, with its principal emphasis on the spirit, has given little attention to the fate of the dead body and has simply asserted dogmatically that, by a miracle, God will somehow reproduce the body at the end of the world. But, as we shall see in the material presented in Chapter One, in many cultures archaic, pagan man has intensively reflected upon the meaning of the body and its decomposition in death, and has assumed the presence of a "mystery" within the corpse, a mystery linked together with the after-death fate of the soul. The alchemists also assumed that this "mystery" was present in their *prima materia*, or in a "subtle body," which they were more interested in exploring than they were in inorganic, perceptible matter. They thought that life's elixir and the secret of immortality were somehow hidden in this "subtle body," which they tried to distill out of tangible material substances.

Henri Corbin's researches have shown that a similar situation to that in Christianity prevails in Islam. There the poverty of the resurrection idea of the Sunnites is compensated for by the rich symbolism of certain Shiite mystics, almost all of which shows historical connections with early Graeco-Egyptian alchemy and with the Gnosis.

Since the dreams of dying people often contain motifs that especially resemble these alchemical-mystical symbols, it seems important to me to take these symbols into consideration, so that we may have before us what are obviously the most natural psychic images of the death process and life after death, spontaneous images which have not yet been consciously shaped into dogma.

The alchemist's preoccupation with the problem of the "subtle body" is fundamentally linked, as we shall see, with ancient Egyptian religious mummification rituals and the liturgy for the dead. For whenever man is confronted with something mysterious, unknown (with the question, for instance, of the origin of the universe or with the enigma of birth) his unconscious produces symbolic, mythical, that is, archetypal, models, which appear projected into the void. The same is also true, of course, with the mystery of death. Such symbols—and they *are* symbols, not to be understood as concrete statements—will be considered here.

In the course of this work, it will become apparent that almost all of the symbols which appear in death dreams are images that are also manifested during the individuation process—especially as it unfolds during the second half of life. As Edinger has remarked, it is as though this process, if not consciously experienced before death, may be "telescoped" by "the pressure of impending death." [11] *In principle, individuation dreams do not differ in their archetypal symbolism from death dreams.*

In his excellent essay "Im Zeichen des grossen Uebergangs" (In the Sign of the Great Passage), Detlef Ingo Lauf has also emphasized this similarity between individuation symbolism and mythical statements about postmortal life. He has shown furthermore that the same archetypes—the basic structures of the psyche that lead time after time to similar symbolic conceptions —seem to be at work over and over again. He cites especially the following structures: a separation of elements in an analogy with creation myths; the motif of the great passage or journey; crossing over water or a bridge, with one or two companions; the re-formation of the dead person in a soul-body or a glorified body;

the weighing or judgment of the soul; the return to another realm of existence; and finally (although not in every system), reincarnation. As we will see, other motifs are to be found. We also find the motifs in different sequences, which is not, in principle, however, of great importance.

In addition to the three above-mentioned areas of inquiry— depth psychology, dreams and alchemical symbolism—we find a fourth area which, as is to be expected, is problematic: we must consider the question, namely, of what extent to take into consideration spiritualism, parapsychological research and modern physics (insofar as the latter is concerned with parapsychology and depth psychology). For me, the mixture of reality and fantasy in spiritualism is something very difficult to sort out. This has been discouraging, even though I do not doubt the genuineness of certain parapsychological phenomena. For this reason I have confined myself to an occasional reference to the *archetypal symbolism* of these phenomena,[12] without discussing the question of their "reality." For the only certainty is that most parapsychological events follow certain archetypal patterns, which can be understood and interpreted psychologically. I cannot conclude, however, whether it is really the dead who respond in spiritualistic séances, or just the complexes of the living participants, or the activated contents of the collective unconscious (the latter happens very often in any case).

It is true that Emil Mattiesen, in his extensive standard work *Das persönliche Ueberleben des Todes* (The Personal Survival of Death), has tried to disprove once and for all the animistic interpretation of parapsychological phenomena (that is, the interpretation of spirits as unconscious split-off egos or, in today's language, autonomous complexes, of the participants in the séances). The present knowledge that we have concerning the unconscious, specifically the collective unconscious, did not exist in Mattiesen's day, so that in part his arguments no longer apply. For we know now that there is a "knowledge" in the unconscious which Jung has termed "absolute knowledge."[13] That is to say, the unconscious can know things which we cannot know consciously, so that all assertions of identity and proofs of the identity of "spirits" in spiritualistic séances could equally well be explained as manifestations of the group unconscious of the participants, as genuine communications from the dead. Only materialization phenomena are not directly affected by this argument. Nevertheless, I "believe" that the dead do manifest themselves occasionally in parapsychological events, although for the time being this does not seem to me to be unequivocally provable.

A similar situation arises in the interpretation of those dreams wherein the dead appear to a still-living person. I will cite some of these in the following pages and interpret them as if they referred, on the objective level, to the postmortal life of the dead person (not to the life of the dreamer). I have had myself certain dreams which Jung interpreted in this way, which at the time was rather astonishing to me. He gave no reason for understanding precisely those dreams on the objective level; he usually interpreted such images on the subjective level, that is to say, as symbols of psychic contents to be found in the dreamer himself. I also was once asked by a woman analyst to study the dreams of a patient of hers, a young girl who had lost her fiancé, a pilot, in an airplane accident. She dreamed of the pilot almost every night, and the analyst and I at first interpreted the dream figure as the image of her own animus, which she had projected onto the fiancé. The unconscious seemed to be suggesting that she withdraw this projection and, by so doing, cure herself gradually of the "loss of soul" suffered through the fiancé's death—that she detach herself from her tie with the dead. But there were six dreams which somehow I could not interpret in this manner. Therefore I told the analyst that in *those* dreams the appearance of the pilot was probably the dead man himself. The somewhat rationally inclined colleague was indignant, asked for a consultation with Jung and presented the whole dream series to him. Without hesitation, Jung (who knew nothing about my choice) picked out the same six dreams and interpreted them on the objective level.

It seems to me that one can "feel" whether the figure of a dead person in a dream is being used as a symbol for some inner reality or whether it "really" represents the dead. It is difficult, however, to set up universally valid criteria for this "feeling." At best it can be said that if interpretation on the subjective level makes little or no sense, even though the dream has an especially strong numinous effect, then interpretation on the objective level might be taken into consideration. This is still an area which is open for further research, since for the time being such questions can be answered only hypothetically.

In this fourth problematic area we also have the question of whether or not there exists a "subtle body" and the related question of whether or not there is a continuous connection between psyche and body, the object of depth psychology and contemporary nuclear physics, respectively. It seems to me, however, that these questions should be broached at the end of this volume, whatever the relevant hypotheses at the present time may be. The reader who does not appreciate them may safely put them aside. For me, they are important because, in the last analysis, they deal with ideas that also concerned the alchemical tradition, namely a universal point of view in which psyche and matter are seen as *one* reality and where death is only partially a separation of "matter" and "psyche." Essentially, however, death would then be a psychophysical transformation.

Finally, it should be noted that many people from middle age on begin to have death dreams. Such dreams do not indicate an immediately impending death, but are rather to be understood as a *memento mori*. They appear for the most part when the ego has an overly youthful attitude toward life and they call for meditation on the part of the dreamer. But only when death has actually occurred soon after such dreams have they been included in this study.

# 1.
# The Mystery of the Corpse and the Grave of Osiris

---

he great difficulty we have in imagining our own life after death, and the difficulty also for survivors to believe in an after-life for the deceased, may well be accounted for by the fact that while still living we identify almost completely with the body. All of our feelings of ego-identity are bound up with the body; these feelings have a long historical tradition and have apparently always been problematic for man.

As we shall see in the following comparative ethnological studies, drawn from many cultures,[1] it has always been difficult for man to free himself of the idea that the dead person is identical with his body. Ethnology therefore speaks of the motif of the "living corpse," for the dead body was at first still treated to a great extent as a living being. In many cultures, for instance those of the Indo-Germanic peoples, the corpse was kept in the house for a month or longer after death.[2] To make this possible, the body was treated with temporary embalming means.[3] The survivors drank, ate, and played in its presence.[4] In other cultures, the corpse was kept in the house or in a relatively shallow grave nearby until it began to decompose, or even until its complete skeletonization, and only afterwards were the remains more deeply buried.[5] It was believed that the soul of the body continued to dwell in the surrounding environment. Some races believe that during this period the dead person, as an incubus or succubus, can even have sexual intercourse with a surviving partner.[6] Even in those cultures where the idea that the dead pass over into a Beyond clearly predominates, customs which look upon the corpse as a representative of the dead person have continued to exist.[7] This is especially apparent in the custom of the so-called "feeding of the dead," which has been widespread among almost all peoples and, to some extent, still is. In many places a tube is put into the grave on a level with the corpse so that the dead body can receive liquid offerings;[8] or for a period of time a hole is left open on a level with the head so that the corpse can "breathe." The belief is that the dead eat the food offerings, and it is claimed that the food presented at the grave or at the funeral meal actually decreases.

A "spiritualization" of this view seems to have spread only gradually, as people began to believe that the dead man lived merely on the "smell" or the "vapor" of the food offerings rather than on the food itself. There is also a Chinese belief that things that the dead require in the Beyond need only be drawn on paper and then burned, so that their image may reach the Beyond with the smoke. In many places the corpse began to be represented during funeral ceremonies by a living person wearing the clothes of the dead. Thus the corpse itself was therefore no longer regarded unconditionally as *the* person of the dead man.

Many peoples make a kind of doll, an image or symbolic construction, to serve as a substitute for the corpse. The Siberian Goldi, for instance, place a white cloth on the bed of the dead person, a cushion with mandala drawings on the cloth, and, in front of it, a wooden picture of Ayami-Fonyalko, the tutelary spirit of the dead, with a burning tobacco pipe stuck in its mouth. All offerings for the dead are then presented to this figure. At one time the Chinese used such a doll for the same purpose, a doll made from a loincloth and called Moon-Go. The Chinese believed that the spirit of the dead person was present in this figure and no longer in the corpse.[9] Koreans, even today, sometimes construct such an image of the dead, just as do the Tibetans. The Japanese also make a *tamashiro*, a receptacle in which the soul of the deceased is carried in the funeral ritual. In China, the ancestors' tablets actually served the same purpose,[10] as did the statue of the dead which the ancient Egyptians erected in the *serdab* (a chamber in the *mastaba* or tomb).

It becomes more or less apparent in observing such customs that the primitive identification of a dead person with the corpse only gradually dissolved as the latter began to be distinguished from some symbol of "concrete identity" (the receptacle). But the dead man obviously had to possess a "body" in order not to lose himself in space or to retain a *pied-à-terre* in case he wanted to visit his family.

Not only were the dead regarded for a long time after death, and over and over again, as identical with the corpse, but often the sense of the whereabouts of the dead man could not be distinguished at first from that of the corpse in the grave. The widespread notion that the land of the dead is full of dust and worms and is clammy and dark indicates an inability to separate the idea of the dead person from the idea of the actual situation of the corpse. Sheol, the Old Testament abode of the dead, is identical in part with the grave in which the dead man lay. Hel, the Teutonic world of the dead, Mictlan of the old Mexicans, and the dismal Hades of the Greeks, to mention just a few, are also characterized by such dark traits.

Later there appeared, in many advanced cultures, a tendency toward a bipartite or multisectional partitioning of man's idea of the Beyond. Common people, evil individuals, and those killed in a specific manner go to such a dark place, whereas certain carefully chosen individuals arrive after death at an extremely pleasant Beyond which is situated above ground. In the dark Hades of modern Greeks, for instance, there are no doctors, priests, or saints, and the ancient Greeks believed that those who had been initiated into the Orphic and Eleusinian mysteries went, not to Hades, but to a glorious Elysium or to the "Islands of the Blessed." Nor did the fallen warriors of the Germanic peoples travel to Hell; they entered Valhalla instead. Aztec warriors and Aztec women who died in childbirth did not go to dark Mictlan, but accompanied the sun across the sky. There is still another special place in the Beyond of the Aztecs for those who were drowned, for those struck by lightning, for lepers, for sufferers from venereal diseases, and for persons who died from fever. These people all went to the verdant Paradise of the rain god Tlaloc.[11]

Sometimes this bipartite or multisectional partitioning of the Beyond is not designed for specific kinds of people but for different parts of the soul of one and the same person. According to an old Chinese view, for instance, the *hun* soul (the male, spiritual or yang element) separates at death from the *p'o* soul (the yin or passive female side). The yang or *hun* soul rises at death and wanders toward the East, while the yin or *p'o* soul sinks to the earth and wanders toward the West. Later they reunite in a sacred marriage at the "Yellow Springs."

According to an old Egyptian view, one part of a dead man's soul, his star-shaped or bird-shaped *ba*, moves freely in space as it follows the bark of the sun god across the sky; whereas the *ka*, a kind of *doppelgänger* or vital soul, is confined to the underworld with the corpse.

Also in other cultures, various "souls" are understood as different psychological aspects of one and the same person. In Hinduism, for instance, man consists of the eternal divine *atman*, which is bound up with the *ahamkara* (everyday ego). Together they form the *jivan*, the individual, which wanders intact throughout many incarnations, while the *ahamkara* changes again and again according to the deeds and thoughts of its previous existence. When the *jivan* has reached the buddhi level (discriminating consciousness), it can enter nirvana and escape the life-death cycle.[12] The *ahamkara* ego is thus in its earthly life more like an earthbound tendency that is constantly changing. The *atman* self, on the other hand, is something permanent. In principle, however, they remain together as *jivan*-person.

Despite such cultural differences—which should by no means be brushed aside—a kind of dualism begins to appear in the understanding of the fate of the dead, a polarity between the idea, on the one hand, of a spiritual realm, free of matter and near to God, in which the liberated "soul" of man floats, and, on the other, of a more matter-bound realm which is associated with a repetition of the life-and-death cycle or which *must be reunited (in a later phase after death) with the free spiritual side*, as for instance the *hun* with the *p'o* in China, or the *ba* with the *ka* in Egypt. Also, wherever the Far Eastern idea of reincarnation prevails, *atman* and *ahamkara* remain together as an ultimate objective; however, one hopes at the end for a total liberation from the downward-moving karmic tendencies of *ahamkara*, so that even in reincarnation all bipartition is eventually terminated.

If we should make an attempt to decide which contemporary psychological concepts best correspond to these two realms of the soul, we must be certain not to fall into a crude equation in which the upper, free soul is equated with consciousness and the lower, "karmic" earth- or body-connected soul with the unconscious. Each seems rather to correspond to different strivings of the primary core, of that totality which Jung calls the Self. The Chinese *hun* soul, the Egyptian *ba*, the Indian *jivan*, etc., seem to correspond to a striving toward becoming conscious, toward awakening, toward detachment from the "world," to a longing for a nearness to God; whereas the *p'o*, the karmic forces, the *ka* soul, etc., strive rather toward a rebirth in this life or toward an effect on their descendants and on the fertility of the earth. A moral evaluation of these two aspirations, either in higher or lower terms, seems to me to be more culture-specific than generally human. The return to life through reincarnation according to the Indian and Tibetan view is, for instance, to be avoided; while for many other peoples close to nature such a return seems to have been *the* natural goal for the dead. The entire death ritual of the Maya, a shamanistic ritual, seems, as far as we understand the texts today, to have served the purpose of providing a path for the souls of the dead to travel to a rebirth within the tribe. For the Maya, the souls of the dead are also the guarantors of the fertility of plants and animals. This is a belief which we also find in many other cultures. The goal is not to float away into a divine spiritual Beyond, but to increase the working of fertility in this life, even by means of a return through reincarnation.

A further polarity appears in the early Christian dispute over the dogma of the resurrection, a polarity between the idea of a *new* spiritual resurrection body and of a restoration to life of the *old* material body. From the Pauline point of view, the dead person, when resurrected, obtains a "pneumatic" body, he resurrects "in Christ" and the question of the restoration of the old body is not specifically mentioned. To a large extent this is still the view of the Eastern church today. Supported by the synoptic gospels, the Western church has preserved primarily an attachment to the idea of the old body of the "corpse," based on the idea that man, having spirit, soul, and body, is a totality and must therefore be resurrected as a totality, as he was before.

An early major advocate of this latter point of view is Tertullian (first half of the third century), who emphasizes in his work *De Carnis Resurrectione* [13] that everyone will be resurrected bodily "in exactly his same flesh." (*Resurget igitur caro, et quidem omnis, et quidem ipsa, et quidem integra.*) This view was predominant for many centuries in the Western churches, as the *Symbolum Quicumque Niceatanun* demonstrates. [14] The sort of concrete forms which this view often assumed in the Middle Ages is seen, for instance, in the serious disputations over whether Christ was circumcised or uncircumcised when he was resurrected, and in discussions about the age of the resurrected body and whether or not it retained all of its former imperfections or was "healed" of them.

If we disregard the concretism of such views, which certainly appears implausible to us today, this adherence to the idea of the old body can be understood plainly as a striving toward preserving the *total individuality* of the dead, their absolute "just-so-ness," which, even during one's lifetime, one automatically equates with the body. *The mystery of the indivisible personality was something which was obviously projected onto the body.*

Now, our conscious ego is by no means only personal, even though we experience it as such when we say "I" (often, at the same time, indicating the body). Numerous impulses, ideas, conceptions, objectives and voluntary actions of the ego are completely collective, that is, they are similar to, if not identical with, those of other people. The same holds true for the unconscious half of the psyche; only one part of its manifestations (dreams, etc.) has reference to some individual experience (that part which Jung called the personal unconscious). A great deal more, however, springs from the collective unconscious and cannot be attributed to the individual. Even that which is most intimate of all, that which we *experience* as "I," as "my" individuality, is in fact many-sided, something which can in no way be exhaustively described in any rational manner. A more conscious realization of these different layers is that gradual process of development through many stages that Jung has called the individuation process. Only when one knows the extent to which he is an endlessly repeatable "human being" in the general collective sense and how far he is limited as an individual, an indivisible, unique being, can one speak of oneself as having become conscious.

In the early Western Christian tradition, which clung to the idea of the "old body" being resurrected, clinging, so to speak, to the corpse of the departed, we can see, on the one hand, a primitive adherence to that original psychic state in which one could not free oneself from the idea that the corpse was still the dead person himself. On the other hand, it seems to me that we have, as mentioned before, a germinal idea lying hidden here, namely that man is an indivisible individual who is meant to survive as a whole. However, only a few of us can still believe today in a concrete reproduction of the old body.[15]

The absurdity of this view would, in any case, be eliminated if, as Jung stresses, we would drop the sense of the "physical-concrete," that is, material, an admonition which would be recommendable for all religious statements. Jung writes:

> "Physical" is not the only criterion of truth: there are also *psychic* truths which can neither be explained nor proved nor contested in any physical way. If, for instance, a general belief existed that the river Rhine had at one time flowed backwards from its mouth to its source, then this belief would in itself be a fact even though such an assertion, physically understood, would be deemed utterly incredible. Beliefs of this kind are psychic facts which cannot be contested and need no proof.
>
> *Religious statements are of this type.* They refer *without exception to things that cannot be established as physical facts.* . . . Taken as referring to anything physical, they make no sense whatever. . . . They would be mere miracles, which are sufficiently exposed to doubt as it is, and yet they could not demonstrate the reality of the spirit or *meaning* that underlies them.
>
> The fact that religious statements frequently conflict with the observed physical phenomena *proves that in contrast to physical perception the spirit is autonomous*, and that psychic experience is to a certain extent independent of physical data. *The psyche is an autonomous factor*, and religious statements are psychic confessions which in the last resort are based on unconscious, i.e., on transcendental processes.[16]

Statements concerning the resurrection of the body must evidently also be understood in this sense, not as something of a coarse material nature. A view of resurrection which comes very near to Jung's symbolic interpretation is found in Origen,[17] who speaks of those people who believe in a *concrete* resurrection of the old body as *simplices* or *rusticos* (illiterates).[18] However, he is also sharply critical of the Docetic view that the resurrected Christ possessed only an illusory body (*phantasma*). His idea of the resurrection body is that neither its matter nor its form will be identical with the old body, but that there does exist *a real continuity of individuality from the one to the other*. As the logos of a tree (the "principle" of the tree) lies hidden in its seed, so does the seed of the resurrection body lie hidden within the old body. This seed is a *virtus*, a *dynamis*, a germ or a germ principle, which Origen characterizes as *spintherismos*, i.e., "emission of sparks." This invisible germ principle in the visible "seed" has substance and is the source of the body's resurrection. It is a "seed-bed" *(seminarium)* of the dead, the ground from which they will rise again. However, the risen body which will spring out of it will no longer be of a coarse material but of a spiritual, even of a divine, nature. It will be invisible to our present eyes and will not be able to be touched by hands. "In that spiritual body the whole of us will see, the whole hear, the whole will serve as hands, the whole as feet."[19] Though the gospels state that Jesus appeared in visible form to his disciples at Emmaus, in tangible form even for Thomas the doubter, Jesus only let it appear that he did so in order to strengthen the faith of his disciples.

This distinctly psychological view of Origen was close to that of many of the Gnostics (his "enemies"), but it did not become generally accepted in the West. St. Augustine, the father of the church, decided in favor of the concrete interpretation, and by the time of Gregory the Great, at the end of the sixth century, this view had acquired almost exclusive acceptance. Only in more recent times has once again an interpretation been heard that is closer to Origen's spiritual view.[20]

Observing from a psychological point of view, one is less surprised by Origen's interpretation of resurrection than by the tenacious adherence of the Western confessions to the concretistic belief. In my view the reason for this lies in the assumption that there is a secret in the concrete body that is not to be abandoned, namely that of the individuation principle. Origen, in his time, recognized that this something was "in the body," but that it was not the body itself. Origen taught in Alexandria, in Egypt, which, in this connection, is important; for the ancient Egyptians were so fascinated by the corpse that they even referred to it as "this secret." The Egyptian *Book of Am-Tuat* (Book of the Other World), which describes the "hidden place" in the world of the dead, states, for instance, in a description of four boxlike graves of gods from which heads emerge: "They are the mysterious figures of Dat (Underworld), the 'boxes' of the earth, the heads of the mysteries. . . . The Lord of the Uas-Scepter and 'she who is provided with the heart' are the guardians of these mysterious images."[21] In the *Book of Hell*, the "box" (coffin) of Osiris is illustrated; he is also guarded by gods who, it

*Fig. 1:* Light and underworld. Above: the earth-god Aker, represented as a double sphinx, carrying the sun-boat, with the sun-god Re in the middle. Below: the mummy under a large sun-disc.

is said, protect his "mystery," that is, as Erik Hornung remarks, his corpse. "You are these gods who guard the property of Dat, the great mystery of the inhabitant of the West (Osiris). . . . I praise (you) when you bow before your mystery, (over) the body of the master of Dat."[22] The sun god Re, when he passes through the underworld, addresses a group of sarcophagi with the following words: "Oh, image of gods in the sarcophagus. . . . Oh, corpse, mightier than magic. . . . Oh, you who conceal the corpses of the gods, he who conceals the body, into which NN[23] has (been) transformed."[24] Or Osiris is invoked: "Oh, Osiris, ruler of Dat. . . . I hasten . . . past in order to see your corpse, your image, which you have hidden under Aker, which is mysterious and unknown."[25] In other parts of the text it is stated of this earth god Aker that he conceals the "great image," i.e., the corpse of Osiris, under his belly.[26] The corpse of Osiris, as well as that of every other dead person (since everyone becomes Osiris after he dies), is therefore something hidden, a "mystery" and at the same time an "image" or "likeness." In my opinion, this indicates that the ancient Egyptians saw something mysterious in the corpse, something which the "image" of the deceased retained, and, as we shall see later, something from which, after the disintegration and transformation of the body, the resurrection process then begins. Therefore, like Origen, the Egyptians believed that resurrection had its beginning in a continuous process out of the concrete dead body, the difference being that with Origen the resurrection process does not begin with the mummy or the "image" in the body, but with that mysterious *spintherismos* (emission of sparks). Origen also refers, as we have seen, to the old body as a *seminarium*, a "seed-plot" out of which the dead grow again. This follows the widespread archetypal idea that the dead return to life, as it were, in the same way that vegetation does. So an image of vegetation very often appears in the dreams of people who are about to die. A man in his forties came to me for a single consultation. He had been given a medical death warrant: melanoma sarcoma with many metastases, a diagnosis which he could not accept. The night after he received this diagnosis, he dreamed the following:

> He saw a green, half-high, not-yet-ripe wheatfield. A herd of cattle had broken into the field and trampled down and destroyed everything in it. Then a voice from above called out: "Everything seems to be destroyed, but from the roots under the earth the wheat will grow again."

I saw in this dream a hint that life somehow continues after death, but the dreamer did not want to accept this interpretation. He died shortly thereafter without having become reconciled with his fate.

This dream motif reminds us of John 12:24: "Truly, truly, I say to you, unless a grain of wheat falls into the earth and dies, it remains alone; but if it dies, it bears much fruit." But what does this saying of Christ mean? How can life develop "out of invisible roots" after death has decomposed the body? After all, what does "wheat" mean?—for obviously it is not meant to be understood concretely, but rather as a symbol. We are able to understand Christ's saying in the Gospel of John only if we place it in its historical context. It alludes to fairly widespread ideas of late antique syncretism, to a time when the symbolism of the Eleusi-

*Fig. 2:* Corn mummy. New grain sprouts from the dead body of Osiris.

nian mysteries, of the festivities of Attis, Adonis and Tammuz, of the Egyptian death rituals and of early alchemy were all more or less universally known.

The oldest alchemical texts of the West had their origin in Egypt and were therefore, from the beginning, imbued with the idea of a life after death; for, as is well known, Egyptian culture was directed toward death and its aftermath to an unusually high degree. The accounts of the Egyptian art of mummification and the liturgy of the dead are the most meaningful documents we have in this respect. One of the oldest Greek alchemical texts, from the first century A.D., is an instruction of "Isis to her son Horus," in which we read the following: "By the permission of a favoring season and according to the necessary movement of the spheres . . . one of the . . . angels who dwell in the first firmament caught sight of (Isis). He advanced towards (her) and wanted to mate with (her) in the intercourse of love." Horus himself was absent and Isis stayed a long time at Hormanouthi, "where the sacred art of Egypt is practised in secret," that is, in the temple of Horus at Edfu. Isis did not submit to the angel but resisted and demanded that he tell her about "the preparation of gold and silver. However, he answered that he wasn't allowed to explain such matters, for this mystery went beyond every description. But the next day ther'd come . . . an angel, his superior, Amnael [presumably the same as Kamephis who, in the text Kore Kosmou, is the same as Kneph-Agthodaimon[27]], and he would be powerful enough to reply to (her) question."[28] His sign would be "a vase that had not been coated with pitch, filled with transparent water."[29] Amnael makes Isis take an oath in the name of heaven and earth, of Hermes and Anubis, of Kerboros (Cerberus) and the ferryman Acheron, never to communicate the mystery to anyone except her son, "so that he might be you, and you he."[30] His instruction is as follows: "Go then . . . to a certain laborer (Achaab) [in another version the ferry-man Acherontos and also Acharantos] and ask him what he has sown and what he has harvested, and you will learn from him that the man who sows wheat also harvests wheat, and the man who sows barley harvests also barley."[31]

Stimulated by this information, Isis, who has begun to reflect upon all of creation, realizes "that it is the condition of man to sow a man, of a lion to sow a lion, of a dog to sow a dog, and if it happens that one of these beings is produced against the order of nature, he has been engendered in the state of a monster and cannot subsist. For a nature rejoices another nature, and a nature conquers another nature." The same is also true of gold and "there is the whole of the mystery."[32] (Recipes for operations follow in the text.)

What does this seemingly absurd text mean? First it speaks of wheat and barley and in so doing implies already what it refers to symbolically. For Osiris, the dead husband of Isis, was referred to as "wheat" and also as "barley," and every dead person is described in the same manner; for according to the old Egyptian view every deceased person becomes the god Osiris at the moment of death. (The corpse and the mummy, as we know, were therefore always addressed as Osiris NN.) Thus, in an Egyptian Book of Aphorisms, the deceased says of himself: "I live, I die. . . . I fall down, the gods live forever, I live in wheat, I grow in wheat which the gods sow, hidden in Geb" (in the earth).[33] Osiris is also called "the Lord of Decay" and "the Lord of the Abundant Green."[34] Or a dead man declares: "I am . . . Osiris. I came from you, wheat. I entered into you, I became fat in you, I grew in you, I fell into you . . . so that the gods live for me. I live as wheat, I grow as wheat, which the sacred ones harvest. Geb [the earth god] covers me. I live, I die, I do not perish."[35]

What this image of vegetation obviously refers to is a *continuation* of the life process, which lasts forever and which is beyond the opposites of life and death. Thus the deceased, in another coffin text, says: "It was Atum who made me wheat, when he sent me down to the earth, to the fire island, when the name Osiris was given to me, the son of Geb. I am life."[36]

As is clear from these quotations, wheat and barley are not to be understood concretely but as symbols for something psychic, something which exists beyond life and death, a mysterious process which survives throughout the temporary blooming and dying of the visible life. This archetypal idea of such a continuing process in nature also appears in a dream that J. B. Priestley relates in *Man and Time*:

> I was standing at the top of a very high tower, alone, looking down upon myriads of birds flying in one direction; every kind of bird was there, all the birds in the world. It was a noble sight, this vast aerial river of birds. But now in some mysterious fashion the gear was changed, and time speeded up, so that I saw generations of birds, watched them break their shells, flutter into life, mate, weaken, falter, and die. Wings grew only to crumble; bodies were sleek and then, in a flash, bled and shrivelled; and death struck everywhere at every second. What was the use of all this blind struggle towards life, this eager trying of wings, this hurried mating, this flight and surge, all this gigantic meaningless biological effort? As I stared down, seeming to see every creature's ignoble little history almost at a glance, I felt sick at heart. It would be better if not one of them, if not one of us all, had been born, if the struggle ceased forever. I stood on my tower, still alone, desperately unhappy. But now the gear was changed again, and time went faster still, and it was rushing by at such a rate, that the birds could not show any movement, but were like an enormous plain sown with feathers. But along this plain, flickering through the bodies themselves, there now passed a sort of white flame, trembling, dancing, then hurrying on; and as soon as I saw it

> I knew that this white flame was life itself, the very quintes-
> sence of being; and then it came to me, in a rocket-burst of
> ecstasy, that nothing mattered, nothing could ever matter,
> because nothing else was real but this quivering and hurrying
> lambency of beings. Birds, men, or creatures not yet shaped
> and coloured, all were of no account except so far as this flame
> of life travelled through them. It left nothing to mourn over
> behind it; what I had thought as tragedy was mere emptiness
> or a shadow show; for now all real feeling was caught and
> purified and danced on ecstatically with the white flame of life.
> I had never felt before such deep happiness as I knew at the
> end of my dream of the tower and the birds.[37]

Priestley understood the flame in his dream as the eternal
cosmic Self, an interpretation which will be discussed below.

The symbol of a life-fire pervading everything visible and
invisible was even more specifically commented on by the Gnostic Simon Magus, a contemporary of the Apostle Peter. Simon,
who was decisively influenced by Heraclitus, taught that the
cosmos consists of fire, one half of which produces the visible
world, the other half the invisible. The latter is an especially
divine fire and "the treasure house of all perceptible and invisible
things."[38] This fire resembles the great tree which appeared to
Nebuchadnezzar in a dream (Daniel 4:7ff), a tree that provided
nourishment for all living things. Its leaves, branches and trunk,
which represented visible life, were eventually destroyed by fire;
however, the fruit of the tree, *which is the human soul*, would not
be burned, but would be brought to the heavenly barn, after
first being purified and freed of its earthly form. *(This fruit is
God's image in the soul.)* The invisible half of the cosmic fire possesses consciousness, whereas the visible fire is unconcious.[39]

This passage states that the incarnated half of the world
energy dissolves and "dies away," whereas an essential part of it,
which is capable of consciousness, i.e., the fruit, continues to
exist. For Simon, this fruit is that part of the human soul which
resembles God's image—in psychological language, a symbol of
the Self. According to the evidence of these images the Self has a
life that survives death or has a form of life that flows through
the universe and, paradoxically enough, somehow flows through
the visible world at the same time.

When, in our alchemical text, the angel Amnael says to Isis

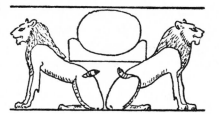

*Fig. 3:* Routi, the Egyptian double lion with the sun-disc, identical with the earth-god Aker. He personifies those earthly processes by means of which the dead return to life.

that the whole mystery lies in understanding that he who sows wheat will also harvest wheat, he alludes to that eternal life which permeates the whole of creation. The next sentence in the Isis text tells us that a lion produces a lion and a dog a dog. This is also an allusion to the resurrection mystery of the Egyptian ritual for the dead, namely to the double lion Routi (Ruti), which is identical with the earth god Aker (mentioned above in our text).[40] This double lion was called "Yesterday and Tomorrow" and was somehow the mysterious agent of the resurrection. He represented the god who personified that incomprehensible process in the earth by which the dead return to life[41] and is at the same time also an image of the human soul. In certain texts he is replaced by two dogs (Anubis).[42] Normally, however, the lion is an image of the sun god Ra who, in this aspect, is addressed as follows: "Radiant by day, lion of his night. He who creates himself within the transformation forms of his name; the nascent one of the becoming."[43] Every resurrected body becomes one with this god.

Looked at psychologically, the double lion symbolizes the double aspect of psychic energy (energy presupposes polarity), whose currents produce an experience of time on the threshold of consciousness. He appears on the borders of the unconscious, where "yesterday and tomorrow" become *one* and in the depths are presumably even suspended altogether.

The text goes on to say that the peasant Achaab, who is also called the seaman Acharantos (in a text variant, Acheron), knows about these mysteries. Many Egyptian coffin or sarcophagus texts refer to a mysterious ferryman who, often after a rigid examination of the dead, moves them across the sky-ocean into the Beyond.[44] In my opinion, the name Acherontos/Acharantos/ Acheron is a combination of the names of the Egyptian god Aker and of Acheron, the Greek river in the underworld, as well as a name for the underworld itself. Aker was regarded as the guardian of the resurrection mystery.[45] He was also considered to be a corpse (mystery) which, as such, guarded "his own image," i.e., the dead body of Osiris.[46] Sometimes he symbolizes the entire realm of the dead or the primal waters of the world's beginning. On a coffin he is represented, like Atum, the all-emcompassing god, as an old man, holding in his hands the egg of the newly risen sun god.[47] In the Book of the Earth the sun god Ra says to Aker: "Oh, you Westerner, who produces the corpses with living forms . . . guardians of procreation, with many forms of appearance."[48] Aker "raises" the dead up high.[49] The great old gods—Atum and Khepri—linger on in him.[50] Underneath him lies hidden the "secret" corpse of Osiris, whom he "guards" during the resurrection process.[51]

These amplifications indicate that in Egypt the mystery of resurrection was related to the creation of the cosmos and of life in general, and that the old alchemists looked for this same mystery in their substance. Wheat (and barley), lion, dog, and the peasant Acherantos are all symbols indicating the continuation and constant renewal of life. The above-mentioned short dream of the trampled cornfield points in the last analysis to something similar.

That the alchemical procedure for the production of the "stone of the wise ones" was understood to have been directly connected with the Egyptian death ritual is shown by a passage from a text of Olympiodorus, an alchemical author who is probably identical with the fifth-century historian of the same name. Olympiodorus describes the mummification (*taricheia*) of the basic substance as follows: When this earthly substance is washed until it is pulverized, one then finds the gold which is present in it.[52] What one finds (the gold) was also called by the ancients by the four-letter (or nine letter) god's name. Obviously, this all deals with the distillation of something divine out of coarse matter.[53]

Later in the text, in describing the same work, Olympiodorus quotes an old oracle which says:

> What is the grave of Osiris? It is a corpse, bound in linen bandages, of which one sees only the face. . . . Osiris is the sealed, air-tight grave which conceals the limbs of Osiris and shows to men only his countenance, but in concealing the limbs it has the effect of amazing (us). He (Osiris) is the source of all moist substances, a prisoner of the spheres of fire.[54]

The fire, which belongs to Seth and to the element lead, is hostile to him because Osiris is water. On the other hand, the sphere of the fire is equated in the same text with water once again.[55] Then the text continues: "But he is now tied together with all of the lead." Of this lead it is later said that "it is so possessed by demons and so obscene, that when the adepts touch it out of ignorance, they go mad."[56]

According to the account in the Egyptian myth, Seth, Osiris' enemy, tricked Osiris into getting into a lead coffin, locked him into it and in this manner caused his death. (That is why Osiris is "tied together" with lead.) The "grave of Osiris"—according to the ancient Egyptians and also in the view of the early alchemists—is the mysterious place whence new life arises once again, a process which at the same time somehow repeats the process of the creation of the world itself. The creation of the world, however, takes place, according to the Egyptians, out of Nun, the primal ocean. Consequently, the "grave of Osiris" in later times was also symbolized by a jug full of water from the Nile, the so-called Osiris Hydreios. Resurrection, therefore, is not a simple matter of restoring the dead body to life, but of a complete reconstruction of it, which, however, had the old body as its point of departure. The Osiris Hydreios is described by Apuleius as the most sacred of the objects which were carried in the Isis procession. It was a round water container with a spout and a handle on which a snake rested. Perhaps this cult object, which is ascertainable only in later times, was derived originally from the Canopic jars, the four jars which concealed the entrails of the deceased. In contrast to these, however, the later vessel contained pure Nile water, the principle of all life and of all life-renewal. J. G. Griffiths emphasizes the fact that the Canopic jars were a symbol of life's continuation: "The themes of the reliefs on the Graeco-Roman type of jar show how this idea is associated especially with Osiris and his circle; *the vessel is a symbol of physical immortality.*"[57] In other words, it is the womb in which the mysterious process of Osiris' rebirth takes place.

I discovered how very much alive this symbol still is today when I heard of the deeply moving dream of a woman who had lost her son when he was young. In this dream, which she had the night after the burial ceremony, she was holding in her hands a small metal box (the urn with her son's ashes), just before it was put into the earth—something which was a great shock for her. The dream continued as follows:

> I was sitting on our sofa at home with a middle-aged woman on my left. She was simply dressed in Victorian fashion, her hair combed backwards with a part in the middle. She was holding a book in her hand and reading aloud from it. She came to a word which I could not understand; it was full of consonants and sounded like "o'-sr-s" I leaned over to see the word in the book. It was "Osiris."

The dreamer associated the woman on the sofa with Madame Curie. She had read recently that in a university, while holding up a milligram of radium given to her as a present, Madame Curie had exclaimed, "For me? Oh, I know a Belgian hospital which needs this very badly!" The small box with a radiumlike substance inside it looked, in the dream, like her son's burial urn. The dreamer concluded, therefore, that the ashes of the body of her beloved son were now supposed to be used to heal the afflictions of others. Seen in this light, the metal box would be the "grave of Osiris," out of which (to use George Fox's words) "the mighty substance of a glorious life would emerge."[58]

What is important here is that *what remains of the body*—in this case the *ashes*—seems to conceal the healing mystery. One is reminded of Origin's idea that the resurrection body is created from "sparks" emanating from the old body. The ancient Egyptians and the early alchemists also believed that resurrection takes place from what remains of the body's *dead matter*, not from the soul alone, but also from transformed matter.

In the above quoted passage from Olympiodorus, the coffin of Osiris is made of lead, a substance which, it is said, can cause madness. It is precisely the darkness, the demonic, that which is hostile toward the dead Osiris, which turns into a "preserving" element and which unites all of the aspects of the individuality into a *principium individuationis,* wherein fire and water seem to be reconciled.[59] Seth's lead, which kills and causes things to dissolve, mysteriously enough also "preserves" the dead from being dispersed within the totality of nature. The following dream, told to me by a sixty-one-year-old cavalry officer, also reminds one of the lead coffin of Osiris. It was dreamed four weeks before the officer's unexpected death from heart failure:

> He was once again in the officers' school where he had acquired the rank of lieutenant thirty years before. An old corporal of whom he thought highly at that time and who in reality had the meaningful name of "Adam," appeared and said to him, "Mr. Lieutenant, I must show you something." He led the lieutenant down into the cellar of the barracks and opened a door—made of lead! The dreamer recoiled with a shudder. In front of him the carcass of a horse lay on its back, completely decomposed and emanating an awful corpse smell.

The simple "mortal Adam" shows the dreamer what is awaiting him, namely the decomposition in death of his animal body, that is, the horse. By means of the shock produced by the dream, the unconscious meant to detach the dreamer from his body, as if to say, "Not you, yourself, but your horse will die." For a cavalry man the horse is, to a special degree, a symbol for that instinctive part of his physical nature which "carries" him. Adam, the universal "simple" man (anthropos) in the dreamer (an image of the Self), knows about the body's impending decomposition and tries to prepare the dreamer for it.

But if we want to be consistent in comparing the dream with the above alchemical text, then we must equate the horse in the lead chamber with the dead Osiris in his lead coffin. The horse would then be not just an image of the body but also an image of the "inner god" in the dreamer (for Osiris represented the "eternal" part in man). In this dream he appears as a horse because the dreamer had never become conscious of this greater aspect of his being; he had been carried through life by the Self without even asking himself what that meant. For that reason his Self remained hidden in the unconscious, in his body, as it were. However, as his relatives discovered afterwards, the night before he died he had secretly placed a crucifix near his bed. Obviously, just at the end, he had had a premonition that the "suffering god-man" was, after all, hidden within the horse. (Osiris is the Egyptian pre-figuration of Christ.)

But let us return to the lead coffin of the alchemists. The resurrection mystery takes place within it, and it is precisely Seth, the demonic element, who plays the role of preserving and saving the deceased. There is an Egyptian gem carving in which Seth is standing on a uterus;[60] he guards, as it were, that which occurs within the womb of rebirth. Seen psychologically, this would mean the following: The demonic in man, the Seth element, is his "evil" autonomous affect, those actions, impulses and emotions which Jung has called the "shadow." They often appear to us also as impulses of the "animal-like," unconscious body. These impulses lock "Osiris" in. This means, for the most part, that they prevent him from becoming conscious of the Self and of individuation. But just at the moment of their apparent victory, at the moment of death, they unite with their opposite, with the principle of good, with Osiris, the water of life, and are transformed in a "vessel" that envelops the Self and makes it possible for the deceased not to fall apart but to preserve his individual identity. The *principium individuationis* is actually related to the devilish element, insofar as the latter represents a separation from the divine within the totality of nature.

Psychologically, we can understand this process as a transformation from egocentrism to ego-consciousness. All of our shadow impulses lead to an egocentrism of desire, of affect, of the impulses of the will. One wants at all costs, and often in a childish manner, to have one's own way. If the ego succeeds in making these impulses conscious and in subordinating them to the Self (to the "god" within), then its fiery energy is transformed into a realization of its identity. The ego then becomes conscious of its "just-so-ness"; the lead coffin, which is felt as confining, transforms itself into a mystical vessel, into a feeling of being preserved and "contained" (also in the sense of no longer being able to lose one's composure).

One of the tragedies of aging—and something which has often preoccupied me—lies in the question of why the aging person, on the one hand, develops a strong tendency to react in a childishly stubborn manner, while, on the other hand, illness and bodily weakness lead him or her into a growing dependency on the tyranny of the medical and nursing staffs of institutions. Without wishing to excuse such tyranny in any way, I ask myself whether a secret meaning does not lie behind this self-deliverance, namely the forcing of precisely this transformation of egocentrism, coming from the shadow, into ego-awareness. At any rate, a ninety-three-year-old woman, who was concerned with the thought of giving up her beloved apartment and moving into a home for the aged, dreamed that in such a home a woman (not the dreamer!) who was hungry for power and who always tried heatedly to have her own way, had to be tamed, that is, to be obliged to give up her power attitude. The demonic lead of the egoistic shadow must be transformed into a "vessel" of ego strength!

Looked at in this light, death could often be seen as a moment when good and evil in the individual collide in a critical manner. In many pictures of the Middle Ages death is represented as a devil and an angel fighting for the soul of a dying person, and the Catholic viaticum also contains traces of an exorcism. The following dream of a patient "who was standing close to death" is from a series of dreams published by Edinger in *Ego and Archetype* and offers an impressive picture of the struggle of the opposites which, in a way, is no fight at all.

> Two prize-fighters are involved in a ritual fight. Their fight is beautiful. They are not so much antagonists in the dream as they are collaborators, working out an elaborate, planned design. They are calm, unruffled and concentrated. At the end of each round they retire to a dressing room. In the dressing room they apply "makeup." I watch one of them dip his finger in some blood and smear it on the face of his opponent and himself. They return to the ring and resume their fast, furious but highly controlled performance.[61]

In the final analysis the fight is described here only as a "spectacle," belonging to the world of illusions. Beyond this struggle, as Edinger points out,[62] lies the Self—the unity of opposites. The dying woman, whose paintings David Eldred has collected, painted a picture with a wrestling match between a light and a dark male figure,[63] again the motif of the collision of opposites. Perhaps we should also see this in connection with the striking and numerous representations on antique sarcophagi of fight scenes, especially duels. We might also recall that in old Rome the gladiatorial battles were originally held in honor of the dead.

The idea that death is a kind of struggle at a decisive moment seems to be of an archetypal nature. Ladislaus Boros, the contemporary Catholic theologian, has dealt impressively with the question of death. From his point of view, death is not a simple separation of body and soul but a complete transformation process, which even has an effect on the inner part of the soul itself.[64] At the moment of death, the inner unity of the soul moves into the world center, into the "heart of the universe" or in the world's core, and there, in a total encounter with itself, decides for or against God. "In this metaphysical place man will make his final decision. What is decided there will exist in eternity . . . [for] now the act becomes being, the decision becomes condition and time becomes eternity."[65] This is a new psychological interpretation of the final judgment and of the assignment of the dead to heaven or hell. "God, in his unchangeable form, becomes for some a martyrdom, for others a bliss, depending on whether in the final decision one rejects the divine love or receives it humbly."[66] It is characteristic of this view, which grew out of the Christian tradition, that the opposites are finally separated, as they are in *Faust* when Mephistopheles is deceived and driven away.

In Egyptian and alchemical symbolism, however, the opposites are *reconciled* at the last moment and remain, in the postmortal body, combined into a unity. This is the reason that, in the Egyptian Book of Gates, at the end of resurrection, the deceased appears as a god with two faces (the heads of Seth and Horus) and accompanies the sun god during his transformation in the underworld.[67] "It is they who announce Re at the eastern horizon of the sky."[68] This figure is called "His Two Faces." It embodies the nature of the opposites which have become one in the deified dead person.

The experiences of dying people are often really very paradox-

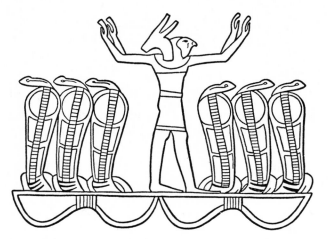

*Fig. 4:* The double-faced god with the heads of Horus and Seth, representing the union of inner opposites in the deified dead.

ical. In some, due especially to a weakening of consciousness toward the end, all kinds of repressed material breaks through. Hans Christian Andersen, for instance, who had remained a virgin all his life, is supposed to have uttered sexual obscenities when he was dying, obscenities so drastically graphic that those who were present fled from the room. Dying people often express a confusion of chaotic impressions. Sometimes, also, relatives are insulted or curses hurled. Some die with this kind of a struggle, whereas others die calmly and with inner peace. In my opinion, these reactions to approaching death represent two aspects of the same process: some are still in agony, in the struggle of the opposites, whereas others seem already to have had a presentiment of the end-result of this fight, the pacification and union of the opposites. The more a person has already been engaged in the struggle of the inner opposites before the approach of death, the more he can perhaps hope for a peaceful end.

# 2.
# The Vegetation:
# Tree, Grass, Corn, and Flower

*I*n the dream motif of the trampled cornfield which grows again and in the wheat and barley symbolism of the dead god Osiris, we have seen that the death of vegetation often appears as an image of human death and, at the same time, as a symbol of resurrection. Thus Edinger's patient, who was at the point of death, dreamed:

> I am alone in a great formal garden such as one finds in Europe. The grass is an unusual kind of turf, centuries old. There are great hedges of boxwood and everything is completely ordered. At the end of the garden I see a movement. At first it seems to be an enormous frog made of grass. As I get closer I see it is actually a green man, herbal, made of grass. He is doing a dance. It is very beautiful and I think of Hudson's novel, *Green Mansions*.[1] It gave me a sense of peace, although I could not really understand what I was beholding.[2]

This green man, like the Egyptian Osiris, is a vegetation spirit. The frog, for which the dreamer at first mistook the green man, reminds us of the Egyptian frog-queen Heqet, who was frequently depicted sitting on the head of a mummy and who represented resurrection. On oil lamps of early Christian graves she unequivocally bears the designation "resurrection." In the Middle Ages, green was considered to be the color of the Holy Spirit, of life, procreation and resurrection.[3] It is the color of a kind of life-spirit or world-soul which pervades everything. As far as the dancing grass man in the dream is concerned, J. G. Frazer[4] and W. Mannhardt[5] report numerous European customs in which a young boy, in springtime or at Whitsuntide, is completely covered with grass or leaves, is ducked into water or otherwise "killed" symbolically, and then rises again. He is called "King May," "the Green George," etc. The event is a magic ritual, designed to bring about the defeat of winter and to insure fertility and sufficient rainfall for the coming year. Sometimes this "Whitsun lout" is replaced by a richly decorated hewn-down tree.[6]

In some places he is also buried, something which was interpreted as a "death-play."[7] Whatever this mythical figure means in itself, it has something to do with death and with life's further blossoming. The American dreamer's dancing grass man must also represent such a May King, an image of the principle of life and death symbolized by vegetation.

Along with grass and grain, the tree also often appears as a symbol for death's mysterious relation to life. Thus, for instance, the aforementioned symbol of the tree made of visible and invisible world-fire (world energy) carried for Simon Magus the sense of life and death united within itself; whereas in the teachings of the Manichaeans, and in keeping with their generally dualistic view of the world, the tree was divided into a tree of death and a tree of life. The former, planted by the demon of desire, ugly and split up within itself, symbolized matter and evil; the latter, however, signified gnosis and wisdom; it is the Tree of Knowledge, whose fruit opened Adam's eyes when he ate of it. At some future time the redeemer will cut down the tree of death, but will plant and preserve the trees of good. The tree of light is also represented as a tree of precious stone.[8]

In the impressive dream series of a young woman dying from cancer reported by Jane Wheelwright, the final dream is as follows: "I was a palm tree, the middle one of three trees. An earthquake was about to occur that would destroy all life, and I didn't want to be killed by the quake."[9] As Wheelwright remarks, the tree is, among other things, a mother symbol. The dream tree therefore represents a devotion to "mother nature." Jung comments on the Germanic legend, according to which man originally came out of trees and will eventually disappear into them again.[10] The world of consciousness yields to the vegetative. The tree is the unconscious life which renews itself and continues to exist eternally, after human consciousness has ceased to exist.

A dying seventy-five-year-old man had the following dream:

> I see an old, gnarled tree high up on a steep bluff. It is only half rooted in the earth, the remainder of the roots reaching into the empty air. . . . Then it becomes separated from the earth altogether, loses its support and falls. My heart misses a beat. But then something wonderful happens: the tree floats, it does not fall, it floats. Where to? Into the sea? I do not know.[11]

In this dream too the tree is certainly an image of continuing life. And the last dream of another man who died a few days later was as follows:

> I am on or in a sky-blue air-liquid that has the shape of an egg and I have the feeling that I am falling into the blue, into the universe. But then it is not so. I am caught and carried by a little blue cloth or by the flakes which hold me. Now I fall into the universe—I want to try it. But I do not lose my hold and I am caught by cloths and by people who speak to me. The small cloths surround me. Red stairways drip and form a Christmas tree.[12]

The blue cosmic air-liquid in the dream will be discussed later. What is important here is the Christmas tree which appears to the dying man as a goal lying in the Beyond. Jung points out in "The Philosophical Tree"[13] that in the alchemical tradition the tree is also considered to be a symbol of the *opus alchemicum*. Psychologically, it symbolizes the individuation process, that is, the continual inner development toward a higher awareness, in which over and over again new lights are seen. Such a tree also exists in the heavenly Jerusalem of the Book of Revelation: ". . . through the middle of the street . . . the tree of life with its twelve kinds of fruit . . . and the leaves of the tree were for the healing of the nations." (Rev. 22:2). In the Islamic paradise there are also numerous trees of precious stones, the most frequent being the so-called tula tree.

> Its root is of mother-of-pearl and its leaves are of silk and brocade. . . . There is no space, no arch, no tree in the garden that could not be shaded by a branch of the tula tree. Its fruits are rare and very much desired in this world, for they certainly do not exist in this world. Its roots are in the sky and its light reaches into every corner of the world.[14]

Here we have an inverted tree; "honorary garments" emerge from its crown for the pious. One may compare this with the little blue cloths in the dream, which protect the dreamer from disintegration. Jung writes about this inverted tree:

The alchemist saw the union of opposites under the symbol of the tree, and it is therefore not surprising that the unconscious of present-day man, who no longer feels at home in his world and can base his experience neither on the past that is no more nor on the future that is yet to be, should hark back to the symbol of the cosmic tree rooted in this world and growing up to heaven—the tree that is also man. *In the history of symbols this tree is described as the way of life itself, a growing into that which eternally is and does not change; which springs from the union of opposites and, by its eternal presence, also makes that union possible.* It seems as if it were only through an experience of symbolic reality that man, vainly seeking his own "existence" and making a philosophy out of it, can find his way back to the world in which he is no longer a stranger.[15]

The dream seems to say to the dreamer that in the Beyond he will continue to grow and to develop toward a higher degree of awareness.

Vegetation symbolism also appears in "Komarios to Cleopatra," one of the oldest texts of Graeco-Egyptian alchemy, dating back to the first century. Before the passage in the text that interests us there is an account of the entire cyclical process through which the "philosopher's stone" or gold is supposed to be produced, a cycle in the form of a mandala of two times four colors and processes (See Fig. 1).[16]

After this general schematization, the text continues:

Observe the nature of plants and from whence they come. Some come down from the mountains and grow up out of the earth, others rise up from caves and from plains. But observe how one approaches them. One must gather them at the right moment, on the appropriate days. Pick them from the islands in the sea and from the upper plains. And observe how the air serves them, how the wheat embraces them protectively, so that they are not damaged or destroyed. Observe the divine water which nourishes them, and how the air rules over them after they have incorporated themselves into one substance.[17]

Before further consideration of the text, I would like to interpolate at this point the brief explanation that the plants discussed here were regarded at the time the text was written as identical

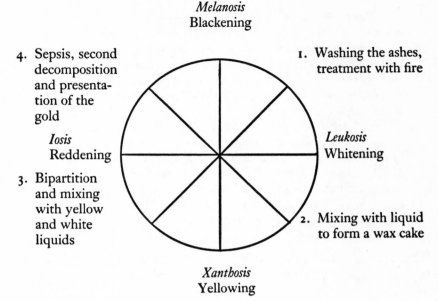

*Melanosis*
Blackening

4. Sepsis, second decomposition and presentation of the gold

*Iosis*
Reddening

3. Bipartition and mixing with yellow and white liquids

1. Washing the ashes, treatment with fire

*Leukosis*
Whitening

2. Mixing with liquid to form a wax cake

*Xanthosis*
Yellowing

There are four principal stages in the alchemical process: *Melanosis* (blackening), *leukosis* (whitening), *xanthosis* (yellowing) and *iosis* (reddening), together with four operations: (1) *taricheia* (mummification and washing), (2) *chrysopoiesis* (production of the gold through fire), (3) *bipartition* and further mixing with white and yellow, (4) *sepsis* (second decomposition, at the end of which the gold appears). The four operations are closely connected with the four color phases.

with certain ores and metals. [18] The two genres apparently differ from each other only in that the metals are "dryer," the plants "wetter." [19] Both grow on mountains and in caves. The ores are considered as "efflorescences" of the earth. Earth, air and water "serve" them and the "wheat embraces them protectively." The trees of precious stones of the Islamic paradise might very well have originated from such alchemical associations.

But back to the text. After an incidental remark, Komarios says to Cleopatra:

> Tell us how the highest comes down to the lowest and the lowest up to the highest, and how the middle approaches the upper and the lower and they become one with the middle, and of what kind of elements they are. And the blessed waters flow down to the dead who are lying there, who are bound and

oppressed in the gloominess and darkness of the depths of Hades. And how life's curing element enters in and awakens them, so that they revive for their creators. And how the new [fresh] waters enter into the head of the grave bed and are born in the bed and come forth with the light and the cloud carries them upward. And the cloud which carries the waters rises up from the sea. When the adepts see this apparition, they rejoice."[20]

Then Cleopatra speaks to the audience:

The penetrating waters revive the bodies and the bound, weakened spirits (pneumata). For they have suffered renewed affliction and have been hidden again in Hades. After a short time they begin to grow and to come forth and clothe themselves in splendid, bright colors, like the flowers in spring. And Spring rejoices and indulges herself in the beauty which clothes them.[21]

I would like to pause here in the Komarios text to consider the psychological meaning of this particular passage. Obviously we have here, in the first place, comparisons drawn from the realm of vegetation. The "ores" blossom like plants from the earth, they die, lie hidden, buried underground, are watered with fresh water, awaken again to life and bloom again with radiant beauty in a new spring.

It is later said of these plants that before reviving they are first "spoiled" by fire. Behind this image there surely lies the pattern of vegetation, which, when cut down by man or dried by the sun, always grows into a physical life again and continues to survive. In the *Vimala Kiuta Sutra*, the body of man is compared to the hardy plantain tree "which has nothing firm in itself. The trunk does die off in the autumn but the creeping root system (the rhizome), which remains in the earth, sprouts anew." Since, however, according to the Buddhist point of view, this new experience is supposed to be interrupted, the image of a radish is often used: one pulls up both its root and branch as a symbol of a definite separation from the wheel of rebirth.[22] However, in cultures where a continuation of life is viewed positively, images of vegetation are to be understood rather as a promise of further existence.

Often the mowing of corn or of grass or the hewing down of trees in the dreams of people close to death also points to the end of life. A fifty-two-year-old analysand of mine had cancer of the bladder which was due for operation. Naturally he was extremely worried about the outcome. He dreamed that an ambulance came to take him to the hospital. (In reality he was still well enough to be able to go by taxi.) The driver got out of the ambulance, opened the back door, and there lay a white coffin. After the operation the patient left the hospital, but only for a short time. Due to metastases he had to return and he died shortly afterward. I cite this brutal dream here because later I will present a very comforting dream of the same man.

As mentioned above, people have frequently objected to my use of consoling dreams on the ground that they are after all only wish-fulfillment dreams. Yet the unconscious usually does announce the end in a highly drastic manner to people who have illusions about the nearness of death, as shown in the above-cited dream of the dead horse, and here in this dream of the white coffin. As a result of this latter dream, the analysand acquainted himself with the possibility of impending death and shortly afterward dreamed the following:

> He was going through a forest in winter. It was cold and misty. He shivered. From a distance he could hear the moan of a chain saw and from time to time the crack of falling trees. Suddenly the dreamer was once again in a forest, but on a higher level as it were. It was summer, sunlight spotted the green moss on the ground. His father (who, in reality, had died long before) walked toward him and said, "You see, here is the forest again. Do not concern yourself any more with what is happening down there" (that is, the hewing down of trees).

The cutting down of trees alludes perhaps to the brutal surgical intervention that awaited him, a damage to and destruction of his vegetative life. (The chain saw is applied to his life tree.) Death here is a woodcutter. In the visual arts he is often represented as a reaper with a scythe. This art motif dates back to the portrayal of the pre-Christian god Saturn, who was often depicted as a harvest god with a sickle. Something is "hewn down" in death, is "cut." Death is always a brutal event, as Jung remarks, and "it is brutal not only as a physical event, but far more so psychically: a human being is torn away from us, and what remains is the icy stillness of death."[23]

The same dream, however, continues on a "higher level" where there is life once again or, in the terms of the dream, there is another forest. In that forest the dead continue to live, as the appearance of the long-deceased father indicates. The mood is happy, agreeable, as in the "new spring" (a description of which appears in the Komarios text), and the dead father advises the dreamer not to worry any longer about what is happening "down there." The unconscious obviously wants to detach the dreamer psychically from the physical terminal event. In reality, the unfortunate man suffered a painful, sorrowful end, which he endured however with great courage. The "higher level" of the second forest could indicate some elevation and intensification of psychic energy, a phenomenon which will be discussed later. The transition from a forest being destroyed to another resurrected forest is established through a typical dream-blending and is not described in any greater detail. The ancient alchemical Komarios text, however, describes more exactly how the plants, that is, the "bodies" and "spirits," suffer the blackness of the underworld and are then awakened and brought back to life by an infusion of the water of life. Then they rise again as spring flowers.

As Henri Corbin[24] has shown, the idea of flowers as *prima materia* is present in the religious conception of the world of the Persians as the primary material of the resurrection process.[25] As we see in Persian landscape representations of the Beyond, every angel and every divine power possesses its own special flower. The god Vohuman has the white jasmine, Shatrivar the basil, the Daena—the divine anima of the male—has the rose of a hundred petals.[26]

One meditates on these flowers in order to constellate their "energies," with which the angel or the divine force itself then illuminates the inner field of vision. Thus the meditation on a flower, as Corbin expresses it, makes possible an epiphany of otherworldly divine beings within the archetypal world.[27]

The idea of resurrection was also for the ancient Egyptians connected with the image of the world of plants and with them,

*Fig. 5:* Vegetative resurrection, symbolized by a blooming lotus flower from which emerges the head of a dead man returning to life.

too, flowers were an aspect of the resurrection body. They even put wheat grains and flower bulbs inside the mummy bandages, or in a container near the dead body and poured water over them. If they germinated, it was taken as a sign of a completed resurrection. Such "wheat mummies" can still be seen in the Cairo Museum. They demonstrate how literally the resurrection of the dead was equated with the germ of either the wheat or of the flowers. This custom also explains an obscure sentence in our text, where we read that "the wheat embraces them (i.e., the plants or the ores) protectively." Here the ore-plants are also identified with the corpse which is wrapped up in the wheat inside the linen mummy bandages.

At the time of resurrection the plants "bloom," as the Komarios text says. Flowers are a widespread archetypal image for postmortal existence, or for the resurrection body itself. In the so-called "vigil hours" of the Osiris mysteries,[28] the "vegetal resurrection" occurs in the fourth hour of the day (to be followed soon afterward by the "animal resurrection," which seems to have been a rebirth rite in which the dead man's *ka* renews itself). Then in the sixth hour it is said that the sky goddess Nut receives the deceased and brings him forth again as a child.[29] The vegetal resurrection is thus the first stage in the resurrection of the deceased, after which the dead man says: "I am that pure lotus flower which emerged from the light radiance which is in the nose of Re. . . . I am the pure flower which emerged from the field."[30] Or he says to Osiris: "I am the roots of Naref, the nehetal plant of the west horizon. . . . O, Osiris, let me be saved, as you let yourself be saved."[31] Or: "I have ascended like the primeval form, I came into being as Khepri (scarab). I have grown as a plant."[32]

In the Far East, the Golden Flower is a symbol of the Self, a familiar image for the eternal in man. Buddha is supposed to have given a wordless sermon at one time, during which he presented a yellow flower (or, according to another version, a white lotus) to his disciples. Only his pupil Kasyapa understood him and responded with a knowing smile.[33] The flower here corresponds to illumination. In "The Teaching of the Pure Land," the flower (the white lotus) is used as a symbol for the man who, in the midst of a guilty, illusive, entangled life, nevertheless "lives in God," in the eternal light and life of the Amidha Buddha. In the Taoistic Chinese text, "The Secret of the Golden Flower," this is described as a "new being," which, through meditation, unfolds from the dark inner depths into silence.[34] It is this unfolding that Jung calls the experience of the Self. At the same time it is also an experience of immortality which has already begun in daily life.[35] "The body resembles the roots of a lotus plant, the spirit is its flower. The roots remain in the mire, yet the flower unfolds toward the sky."[36] The golden flower represents a union with the "ever creative One";[37] immortality lies within it,[38] so that an eternal or dharma body may thereby be crystallized.[39]

Today in Nepal flowers and grains of rice are still scattered on cremation pyres. During celebrations for the dead, garlands of *tagetes* (yellow flowers) are strung over the sacred river to make a bridge to the Beyond. The so-called *tulasi* flower also plays a special role. An infusion from this flower is given to the deceased to drink and its leaves are placed on his tongue. When a member of the warrior caste dies, *tulasi* flowers are placed in front of the corpse and pieces of its roots are laid on the tongue, ears, eyes, and top of the head. Water from the Ganges is blown over him while the name of the flowers—*tulasi*—is called out three times. In this way his soul can escape into the sky. Furthermore, after death the soul can still visit its survivors by descending from the house altar over *tulasi* flowers.[40] Orange-yellow *tagetes* are still used by the Indians in Guatemala as a symbol of All Saints Day; for them the flowers represent sun, light and life.[41]

The West does not possess such highly differentiated views of the nature of this soul-flower as does the East, but the idea does appear frequently as an archetypal motif. For instance, in "The Vampire," a Gypsy fairy tale,[42] a pretty, innocent girl is pursued by a vampire-like devil and, after vain attempts to escape, is killed. A flower, "which shines like a candle," grows up on the head of her grave. The emperor's son rides by, picks the flower and takes it to his room. At night the girl emerges from the flower and sleeps with the prince; in the daytime she is once again transformed into the flower. The prince is weakened by these nocturnal adventures, until his parents discover the secret and seize the girl. The son awakens and is finally united, while awake, with the beloved. She gives birth to a golden boy who holds two apples in his hands. But, after a while, the vampire returns and kills the child. The girl warns the vampire that "he may die wretchedly," whereupon he explodes. She tears his heart from his body and with it brings the child back to life.

As in Eastern mysticism, the flower is here a symbol of absolute inner unassailability, and of life that survives death. The golden boy, which the heroine bears, is, like the flower, an image of the Self, but more human and therefore more vulnerable to the devil. Only the heroine's bravery is eventually able to conquer the destructive principle.

The motif of survival as a flower on the grave is also quite common in legends. In Swiss folklore, for instance, a story is told of the attempt, in the year 1430 in Hiltisrieden, to build a curate's house. A lily sprang from the earth, where it had grown through the heart of a corpse that rested on that spot. Later the same story was told of the place nearby, where Duke Leopold was buried, and it was said that the lily had grown from his heart. The Swiss saint Nicholas of Flüe once, while deep in prayer, had a vision in which he saw "a white lily with a wonderful fragrance spring upward out of his mouth until it touched

*Fig. 6:* In a Mayan ritual, the soul of the departed is accompanied on his journey to rebirth by the bird Moan (center) with the words, "Living grain," on its beak, and (right) a god with a long seed-stick.

heaven." (At the same time, he thought about his cattle, and his favorite horse ate the lily.) Here the lily is obviously a subtle-body apparition, an image of Nicholas' *anima candida* which strives toward heaven.[43]

The flower is thus an image of the soul, which frees itself from the coarse material of the body; at the same time it is an image of the post-mortal existence of the soul.[44]

In the culture of the Maya, the growth of vegetation was also closely associated with the cult of the dead.[45] The decipherment of the Mayan script is unfortunately still very uncertain; therefore I can point to only a few of the more general characteristics.

The Maya seem to have practised a ritual in which they accompanied the soul of the departed into the Beyond, from the moment of his death until his rebirth. "The souls of the dead had a close relation to the life of plants, especially of corn. They also assisted plants in their rebirth."[46] Not everyone, however, took part in this kind of initiation. Some individuals disappeared into gloomy Mictlan, never to return. Fallen warriors, on the other hand, and women who died in childbirth entered the heavenly regions and accompanied the sun on his journey until evening. Then they returned to the earth as butterflies and hummingbirds. Upon dying, the deceased was confused at first, but with a priest's help he was awakened and became active again. He lost his body, but as an "eye" or a "soul" he chose a pregnant woman in whose child he could return to life.[47] The ideogram for this re-procreation is a vessel full of ashes (!), or a little bone from which two or three leaves are growing.[48] A bird named Noan, with the words "living grain" on its beak, helps the soul to its rebirth.[49] Paul Arnold, editor of the Mayan Books of the Dead, points to the close relationship between these ideas and those of the ancient Chinese.

In ancient times the Chinese probably buried their dead on the north side of the house,[50] where the grain for the next sowing was kept. Originally, they thought that the dead somehow went on living in the ground water under the house, near the Yellow Springs which marked the end of their journey. From the Springs they returned to life.[51] Marcel Granet informs us that

> the Yellow Springs formed the land of the dead, a reservoir of life; because the Chinese were of the opinion that the Yang, which had withdrawn into the Yellow Springs in the depths of the north (the depths are yin) survived the winter (yin) enclosed and surrounded by the Yin (water). There it won back its full power and prepared itself . . . to burst forth anew.[52]

It began to grow again at the winter solstice.

Later the dead in China were buried in tombs north of the city. The north is associated with the time of winter rest and with the festival in commemoration of the dead. In this festival, players wearing animal masks wandered around, presenting themselves as the spirits of the dead, and people went to the burial places to repair them.[53] They also had a ceremonial meal to which the spirits of the ancestors were invited.[54] This was followed by the clearing of the fields, the plowing, and the first sowing.[55] This was also the time for weddings, another sowing of new life.

The Chinese believed that their ancestors returned to life in their descendants, not as identical persons but as their intimate life essence, which was also that of the family.[56] Hence there is a mystical analogy between the dead, who go into the earth for a winter's rest, and the grain which rests in the northern, storage-room side of the house and awakens again to new life in spring. In the West, too, in the Mediterranean area, especially in late Mycenean times, the dead were often buried in so-called *pithoi*, earthen storage vessels in which grain was otherwise kept. As the grain, sown in spring, awakens to new life, so will the dead, too, arise again in the Beyond.[57]

Again and again we read in the literature that the "vegetation gods" are associated with resurrection symbolism, in the sense that Osiris, Attis, Tammuz and others *signified* the death and rebirth of vegetation. Seen psychologically, this is incorrect. For rural cultures, vegetation in its concrete aspect was no mystery but such an intimate part of their lives that it was not in itself divine. In the cult of the dead it served rather as a symbol for something unknown, something psychic, and like all archetypal symbols was therefore closely interwoven with many other mythical images. Vegetation represented the psychic mystery of death and resurrection. Moreover, one should bear in mind that in reality all vegetation is characterized by the fact that it draws its life directly from so-called dead, inorganic matter, from light, air, earth and water. For this reason it is an especially appropriate symbol for the miracle that out of "dead," gross substances new life can arise. Now, man's dead body also consists of inorganic matter only, and indeed—or so one hopes—a living "form" could arise from it again, as the vegetation imagery indicates.

Unlike the tree, grass, and bunches of flowers, the symbol of a single flower has a particular meaning. Flowers are generally mandala-shaped (Buddha's golden flower!), which makes them especially appropriate as a symbol of the Self. So the mythos of the flower would suggest that in the flower the Self possesses or builds for itself a new mandala-shaped body insofar as it extracts its "life essence" from the dead body.

Our rich offerings of flowers and wreaths of flowers at a burial surely symbolize not only our feelings of sympathy but also, *unconsciously*, a "resurrection magic," a symbol for the return of the departed to a new life; to this belongs also the mandala form of the wreath.

How alive the flower is as a symbol of the postmortal "body," as a firm abode for the soul, I discovered to my sorrow through the "active imagination" of a fifty-four-year-old woman, an analysand and friend of mine, who died unexpectedly. Active imagination, as we know, is a form of meditation taught by Jung, in which one conducts a conversation with inner fantasy figures. In her imagination, the conversational partner of this woman was a spiritual bear man. The layman can imagine him as a kind of inner guru.

One month before her death, she wrote the following "imagination":

I:    Oh, my big bear! I am so cold. When will we get to our homeland?

Bear: You will only really be there at your death.

I:    Can't we go there now?

Bear: No. You must complete your tasks first.

I:    I can't because I am so cold.

Bear: I will give you my animal warmth.
    (He embraces me carefully and slowly warms me up again.)

I:    Can't we go now, for just a short visit, to that beautiful homeland?

Bear: It's dangerous.

I:    Why?

Bear: Because one does not know for certain whether one will return or not.

I:    Haven't we already stood here more than once before . . . in front of the wonderful flower?[58]

Bear: Yes, but that is not the same as entering it.

I:    But I cannot live without this center. The center must always be with me. I do not want to be outside, but always inside it. Outside, everything is meaningless, one is left to chance.

*Six days later.* I see the flower. It shines, radiantly wonderful, in the dark forest. It has grown; it is rooted and is eternal. Its radiant bloom has eight leaves, four golden and four silver, distributed symmetrically. It is in the center of a circular area, surrounded by a thick, high wall which has four locked gates.

My companion, the bear, has four golden keys. He opens one of the gates. We enter. He locks the gate behind us. As soon as I am inside the wall, I feel very well.

I: Why do I feel so well here?

Bear: Because there are no demons inside the wall.

I: I am very happy in our homeland, in the center. The flower radiates a wonderful healing light. I am not in the flower yet, but I am near it, in its protection, in its mild warmth. It is inner order, the center. There is no splitting here, no halfness.

*A few days later.* Here, near the flower, I am safe from too much heat or cold.

I: Why is the wall so thick?

Bear: To protect us against God.

I: Who built it?

Bear: God.

I: Who arranged for the flower to grow?

Bear: God, in order to protect you against him.

I: Terrible, awful, kind, helpful God!

*One week later.* The mystery of the flower is within me. I am it and it is me. It has entered me and has been transformed into a human being. . . . I *am* this radiant flower, from which a spring has burst forth. . . . Am I this? From now on, when I go to the flower, I know that I go into myself.

*Two weeks later.* I go to the wall. My companion, the bear, opens one of the four gates for me. We enter. . . . As soon as we are inside the surrounding walls he takes on human form. He wears a golden coat. I look at the flower. As I meditate on it, *I am transformed into a flower, fully rooted, radiantly eternal. Thus I take the shape of eternity.* This makes me quite whole. . . . As flower, as center, no one can harm me. I am protected in this way. For the greater part of the time I will have to return to human form, but again and again it will be possible for me to become the flower. I am happy about this, for until recently I did not know it was possible. I only knew the flower as an object. Now I know that I can also *be* it.

The text ends here abruptly, for shortly afterward the writer died, quite unexpectedly, from a lung embolism. It was as though she definitely wanted to go inside the flower, clearly a symbol of the postmortal body.

This does not mean that the resurrection body actually resembles this flower form. One must of course understand the flower as a *symbol* for a form of existence, that is in itself unimaginable and not rationally understandable. As stated in the Jungian view, the mandala structure of the flower points to the Self, the inner psychic totality. In this sense the flower is a slowly maturing inner core, a totality into which the soul withdraws after death. In one passage of the active-imagination exercise not given here, the writer also calls the flower a star. This is another historically familiar symbol for the resurrection body. In ancient Egypt, the immortal *ba* soul, as we have seen, was represented as a bird or as a star. The star symbolizes the eternal uniqueness of the dead man who possesses his own identity as one among millions of stars. This motif occurs later in our principal text, the Komarios tractate, to which we must now return.

# 3.
# The First Death Marriage

*I*n alchemy, the revival of "plants" (ores) through watering was also understood as a wedding. The Komarios text continues as follows:

10. But I say to those of you who are well-disposed: When you preserve the plants and elements and ores (stones) in their proper place, they *seem* indeed to be very beautiful, but they are not beautiful when the fire tests them. (Later) when they have taken on the glory of the fire and its shining color, then you will see how their glory has increased when compared with their former glory, inasmuch as the desired beauty and its fluid nature have been transformed into divinity. Because they (the adepts) nourish them (the plants) in fire, just as an embryo is nourished and grows rapidly within the womb. But when the month of delivery approaches, then it (the embryo) is not prevented from coming forth. Our sacred art (the art of alchemy) proceeds in the same way. The constantly billowing tides and waves wound them (the bodies) in Hades and in the grave in which they lie. But when the grave is opened, then they come forth from Hades, like the child from the womb. When the adepts observe this beauty, like a loving mother observing her child, then they look for ways in which they can nourish the child (the corpse) in their art, (that is), with water instead of milk. For the art imitates child(birth), since it is also formed like a child, and when it is completed in every way, you will behold the sealed mystery.

11. Now I will clearly inform you as to where the plants and elements are. But I will begin with a parable (*ainigma* also means "riddle"): Go to the highest place in the forest-covered mountains and at the very top you will find a stone. Take the male element (*arsenikon*) from the stone and whiten it in a divine manner.[1] Then look at the middle part of the mountain, below the place of the masculine; there lies the female companion with whom he will become one and in whom he rejoices. For nature rejoices in nature; otherwise she does not become one. Go down to the Egyptian Sea, taking with you the so-called Nitron, which comes from the source, the sand. Unite them there with each other, and this union will (then) produce the multicolored beauty; without this beauty they will not become one. For the dimensions of the male are the same as those of

41

his female companion. See, nature rewards nature, and when you have brought everything together in harmony, then natures overcome natures and they rejoice in each other.

12. Look, wise ones, and understand; observe the fulfillment of the art through the bringing together and union of bridegroom and bride. Observe the plants and their differences. I say to you: See and understand that out of the sea the clouds arise, and the clouds carry the blessed waters with which they water the earth and from the earth spring forth seeds and flowers. Thus our cloud, which rises from our element, also carries divine water and waters the plants and elements and needs nothing which comes from other places.

13. Observe the paradoxical mystery, brother, the great unknown; observe how obvious the truth is to you. Observe and water your earth and be careful how you nourish your seeds, so you will be able to harvest the most beautiful fruit. Hear now and understand and take carefully into account all that I say. Take from the four elements the highest masculine and the lowest, that which shines white and reddish, masculine and feminine, of the same weight, in order to combine them with each other. For just as a bird warms and hatches its eggs with its incubation heat, so you, too, warm and release *(leiosi)* (them) and bring them out, watering them with divine waters in the sun and in hot places and cooking (them) over a mild fire in the milk of virgin women and watching out for the smoke.[2] Chain them, that is, in Hades and guide them forth again, steep them in Cilician crocus in the sun and in hot places and cook them in the milk of virgin women in mild warmth, safely away from the smoke, and chain them in Hades and move them with care until their preparation has become more stable and they can no longer escape the fire. Then take them out and when the soul *(psyche)* and spirit *(pneuma)* have become *one*, then project it (the one) onto the body of the silver and you will have gold, such as kings in their treasure houses do not possess.[3]

A description of the actual resurrection follows this passage in the text. But first we must examine some of the above motifs more carefully. There is something new in Section 13: the description of a union of upper and lower in the form of bridegroom and bride. This motif is only more or less hinted at here, whereas in later alchemical texts it gains more and more prominence. It represents *the* union of the psychic opposites, a union which Jung has described in his extensive work, *Mysterium Co-niunctionis*. This *hierosgamos* (sacred marriage) is a "death wedding," also a commonly widespread archetypal motif.

Jung himself had such an experience of the *hierosgamos* while in a near-death state, which he has described in his memoirs. He had survived three heart and lung embolisms but was still hovering between life and death:

> By day I was usually depressed. I felt weak and wretched. . . .
> Toward evening I would fall asleep, and my sleep would last until about midnight. Then I would come to myself and lie awake for about an hour, but in an utterly transformed state. It was as if I were in an ecstasy. I felt as though I were floating in space, as though I were safe in the womb of the universe—in a tremendous void, but filled with the highest possible feeling of happiness. . . .
>
> Everything around me seemed enchanted. At this hour of the night the nurse brought me some food she had warmed—for only then was I able to take any. For a long time it seemed to me that she was an old Jewish woman, much older than she actually was, and that she was preparing ritual kosher dishes for me. When I looked at her, she seemed to have a blue halo around her head. I myself was, so it seemed, in Pardes Rimmonim, the garden of pomegranates, and the wedding of Tifereth with Malchuth was taking place.[4] Or else I was Rabbi Simon ben Jochai, whose wedding in the afterlife was being celebrated. It was the mystic marriage as it appears in the Cabbalistic tradition. . . . I do not know exactly what part I played in it. At bottom it was I myself: I was the marriage. And my beatitude was that of a blissful wedding.
>
> Gradually the garden of pomegranates faded away and changed. There followed the Marriage of the Lamb, in a Jerusalem festively bedecked. . . . These were ineffable states of joy. . . .
>
> That, too, vanished, and there came a new image, the last vision. I walked up a wide valley to the end, where a gentle chain of hills began. The valley ended in a classical amphitheater. It was magnificently situated in the green landscape. And there, in this theater, the *hierosgamos* was being celebrated. Men and women dancers came onstage, and upon a flower-decked couch All-father Zeus and Hera consummated the mystic marriage, as it is described in the *Iliad*.
>
> All these experiences were glorious. Night after night I

floated in a state of purest bliss, "thronged round with images of all creation." Gradually, the motifs mingled and paled. Usually the visions lasted for about an hour; then I would fall asleep again. By the time morning drew near, I would feel: Now gray morning is coming again . . . ![5]

For Jung the return to the everyday world was enormously difficult and depressing. He describes this experience further in a letter: "Throughout my illness something has carried me. My feet were not standing on air and I had the proof that I have reached a safe ground. Whatever you do, if you do it sincerely, will eventually become the bridge to your wholeness, a good ship that carries you through the darkness of your second birth, which seems to be death to the outside."[6]

St. Thomas Aquinas died in a state of ecstasy as he was interpreting for the monks of St. Mary at Fossanova the Song of Solomon—certainly the most beautiful representation of the *hierosgamos* in Western tradition. Thomas was supposed to have died as dawn was breaking, at the words *"Venite, dilecti filii, egredimini in hortum."*[7]

The alchemical treatise *Aurora Consurgens* probably has its origin in this interpretation of the Song of Solomon by St. Thomas. In the *Aurora* the Bride speaks:

> I stretch forth my mouth to my beloved and he presseth his to me (cf. Song of Songs 1:2); he and I are one (cf. John 10:30); who shall separate us from love (cf. Romans 8:35-39)? None and no man, for our love is strong as death (cf. Song of Songs 8:6).[8]

The Bridegroom answers:

> O beloved, yea supremely beloved, thy voice hath sounded in my ears, for it is sweet (cf. Song of Songs 2:14), and thine odour is above all aromatical spices (cf. Song of Songs 4:10). O how comely is thy face (cf. *ibid.* 4:11), thy breasts more beautiful than wine (4:10), my sister, my spouse, thy eyes are like the fishpools in Heshbon (7:4), thy hairs are golden, thy cheeks are ivory, thy belly is as round as a bowl never wanting cups (7:2), thy garments are whiter than snow, purer than milk, more ruddy than old ivory (cf. Lamentations 4:7), and all thy body is delightful and desirable unto all. Come forth,

daughters of Jerusalem, and see, and tell and declare what ye
have seen; say, what shall we do for our sister, who is little
and hath no breasts, in the day when she shall be wooed? (Song
of Songs 8:8-9) I will set my strength upon her and will take
hold of her fruits, and her breasts shall be as the clusters of the
vine (cf. Song of Songs 7:8). Come, my beloved, and let us go
into thy field, let us abide in the villages, let us go up early to
the vineyard, for the night is past and the day is at hand (cf.
Romans 13:12); let us see if thy vineyard flourisheth, if thy
flowers have brought forth fruits. There shalt thou give thy
breasts to my mouth, and I have kept for thee all fruits new
and old (cf. Song of Songs 7:11-13); . . . let us fill ourselves
with costly wine and ointments, and let no flower pass by us
save we crown ourselves therewith . . . let us leave everywhere tokens of joy, for this is our portion (cf. Wisdom of
Solomon 2:5ff), that we should live in the union of love with
joy and merriment, saying: Behold how good and pleasant it is
for two to dwell together in unity (cf. Psalms 132:1).[9]

The alchemists understood this text as a description of the completion of their opus. It is, at any rate, a description of the completed individuation process, of an ultimate union of psychic
opposites, a liberation from all egocentricity and an ecstatic
entrance into a state of divine wholeness.

The wedding motif appears not only in such ecstatic experiences at the end of life, but also in dreams which point to an
impending death. An elderly retired nurse, for instance, wrote
to me that she had dreamed of receiving an announcement of her
engagement or betrothal to which she fully consented without
knowing who her fiancé would be. When she awakened she was
unable to make anything of the dream. Then she fell asleep again
and dreamed that "she was in a white death dress, holding a red
rose in her hand. She walked toward the bridegroom, her heart
full of desire and joy." Upon waking she realized that the bridegroom must have been Jesus Christ and that the dream's purpose
was to prepare her for approaching death.

Edinger reports the following dream of the patient who, when
about to die, had dreamed of the "dancing grass man":

There is a darkness, but with a luminosity in it, not describa-
ble. A darkness somehow glowing. Standing in it is a beautiful

golden woman, with an almost Mona Lisa face. Now I realize that the glow is emanating from a necklace she is wearing. It is of great delicacy: small cabochons of turquoise, each circled in reddish gold. It has a great meaning for me, as if there were a message in the complete image if only I could break through its elusiveness.[10]

Edinger compares this anima image with the Biblical figure of Sophia, who embodies the sum of the eternal archetypal images (the precious stones), the *sapientia* through whom God, according to a medieval idea, "knows himself."[11] She is a cosmic spiritual force, which, in this instance, obviously approaches the dreamer as a messenger of death.

Some years ago a fifty-two-year-old married doctor came to me for analysis. He was physically and psychically in good health, but his general medical practice had begun to bore him and he wanted to be trained to become a psychotherapist. His initial dream, however, pointed unexpectedly to something quite different. (We consider the first dream brought to an analysis as having particular importance, for very often it outlines in advance the entire course of the analysis.) This doctor had dreamed:

He was going to the funeral of some man who had been indifferent to him; he was just walking with a lot of people in a funeral cortege. In a little square place in the town, where there was a green lawn, the cortege stopped. On the lawn there was a pyre and the bearers laid the coffin on it and set fire to it. The dreamer watched it without any special feelings. When the flames sprang up, the lid of the coffin opened and fell off. Out of the coffin sprang a most beautiful woman; she opened her arms and went toward the dreamer. He too opened his arms to embrace her and woke up with a feeling of indescribable bliss.[12]

I was frightened when I heard this initial dream. It seemed to me that its purpose was to prepare the dreamer for approaching death, and yet he was so young and energetic. Especially sinister for me was that feeling of "indescribable bliss." Following this dream, however, the doctor had "normal" dreams once again, and the analysis took its "normal" course. After a year of analytic work, the dreamer, for financial reasons, had to return to his own country, but with the intention of coming back soon to finish his training analysis. Then, out of the blue, I received news of his death. He had caught influenza, it had become rather serious, and he had died from a heart attack in the ambulance which was taking him to the hospital.

Now let us look more closely at the dream. First there is the funeral of an indifferent man. He probably represents the dreamer's earthly, bodily aspect, which in death has become a stranger, someone indifferent, the "old Adam" whom he had discarded. This figure corresponds to the decomposing horse in the dream of the cavalry officer described earlier. From the Jungian point of view, the square field represents a mandala, an image of the Self, of the completed personality. Grass is growing there, an allusion to vegetation as a resurrection symbol. The coffin is put into a fire. This motif, which will be discussed later, presumably refers to the *psychic* background of early cremation customs, for it pictures a kind of cremation which does not occur in crematoria today, but takes place in a green field of mandala form.

Instead of a dead man, a beautiful naked woman comes unexpectedly out of the coffin. She represents the dreamer's anima, his unconscious feminine side. She must have emerged, through the effect of the fire, from the man's dead and cremated body. This is what the alchemists would call the *extractio animae*. This "extraction of the soul" is also described in the Komarios text, which I have chosen as a guide text for the present section of this study. In the "fire treatment" the soul (psyche) abandons the dark, ill-smelling corpse, springs forth as a "cloud," and, like rain to the earth, comes back again to the body.[13] This return is the sacred marriage of psyche and body in the Komarios text and —in the above dream—the marriage of soul and dreamer (the latter having gotten rid of his indifferent corpse).

Jung points out that the anima strives at first to involve a man in the business of living, but toward the end of life, when she has been integrated, she becomes a mediatrix to the Beyond, to the contents of the unconscious. She then acquires a spiritual-religious aspect. She becomes, for him, Sophia.

The young woman with cancer, whose dream series Jane
Wheelwright has reported, dreamed the following initial dream,
the most important dream of her analysis:

> I came upon a Sumerian tower with great ramps zigzagging to
> the top. It was also Southern California State College, over-
> looking the University of Southern California. I had to climb
> to the top; it was a horrifying ordeal. When I got there I looked
> below, and throughout the city I saw buildings from the
> Sumerian, Romanesque, Gothic, and ancient Indian eras.
> There was a large, elegant book lying open before me. It was
> handsomely illustrated with architectural details of these build-
> ings, of their friezes and sculptures. I awakened, terrorized by
> the height of the tower.[14]

In Wheelwright's interpretation of this dream, she reminds us
that the Sumerian ziggurat was regarded as the center of the
world, and also as the world-axis connecting sky and earth. In
the dream it is an image of the Self. Obviously the dreamer must
reach a much higher level of consciousness before she can die;
and she must also get a glimpse of the great impersonal historical
aspects of the psyche, of the values of the collective unconscious
and of the secular processes in the history of the development of
the human mind. In Sumeria, high up on the ziggurat, the goddess (personified by the priestess) celebrated the *sacred marriage*
with her son-beloved, the image of a union of cosmic opposites.
Thus the first dream, through its allusions, already reveals the
final goal of individuation—the *hierosgamos*—even though this
can be deduced only indirectly from the amplification of the
image of the ziggurat.

In general we have few reports in literature of the death-
marriage motif in cases of women. This is probably to be
accounted for, in the first place, by the fact that the literature
known to us has for the most part been written by men. But the
motif of the death animus does exist in literature, especially
familiar through G. A. Bürger's "Leonore":

> *Wie scheint der Mond so hell,*
> *Die Toten reiten schnell,*
> *Feinsliebchen graut dir nicht?*[15]

*How brightly the moon shines,*
*The dead ride swiftly,*
*Are you not afraid, my love?*

Less gloomy is the death bridegroom who appears in Schubert's "Death and the Maiden" (op. 73). There Death says to the frightened girl:

*Bin Freund und komme nicht zu strafen.*
*Sei guten Muts! Ich bin nicht wild;*
*Sollst sanft in meinen Armen schlafen.*[16]

*I am a friend, I have not come to punish you.*
*Be brave! I am not a wild man;*
*You will sleep gently in my arms.*

Finally, there is also a type of fairy tale in which a woman marries death, personified as a human being. Thus, for instance, in a Gypsy fairy tale, we are told of a beautiful young woman who lives all alone. Her father, mother, brothers, friends are all dead. Once a handsome wanderer comes to her dwelling and asks for lodging, for "in a thousand years he has slept only once." He stays with her a whole week and she falls in love with him. One night he appears to her in a dream and later she tells him of this dream. "You were so cold and white and we rode in a beautiful carriage. You blew a big horn. Suddenly all of the dead approached and followed you, for you were their king and you wore a beautiful fox coat." The wanderer replies, "This is an evil dream," and says that he must leave her now, "for no one in the world has died for a long time." The young woman forces him to reveal who he is. The wanderer says, "Good, then you must come with me, I am Death." The young woman is so frightened that she dies.[17]

In "The Wife of Death,"[18] a Breton story, Margarethe, a lonely woman who is already over 40 years old, marries an unknown stranger who suddenly appears out of nowhere. He takes her away with him, bidding her say farewell to her young brother, who is also her godson, and to tell him that he should visit them sometime. They wander toward the sunrise for many months until they finally reach a building with high walls. This is the "Castle of the Rising Sun," their home. Margarethe has everything she wishes there, but during the day she is lonely waiting for her husband to return. The rest of the story concerns the experiences of the godson who visits her and accompanies Death on his mysterious daily path in the Beyond. Such a day's journey, however, lasts 500 years, so the brother can never again return home but must remain in the other world. He observes that Death, both on his arrival at the castle and on his departure, slaps Margarethe three times on the face. When the godson asks Margarethe about this, she tells him that the slaps are kisses (!). (It seems as if a revaluation of feeling-values takes place in the Beyond, something which is in accordance with the fact that some peoples depict the realm of the dead as a reversed world where people stand on their heads.)

We should also mention here the figure of the large "cosmic shepherd" or "fencing master," even though no marriage is mentioned. He appears in the martyrology of Passio Perpetuae et Felicitatis, where, in a dream he offers the condemned Perpetua a communion offering of cheese and milk; then, in a second dream, golden apples.[19] No marriage takes place with him; generally, however, as mentioned above, the incidence of the death-wedding motif for women is far less than for men.

The symbolism of the death wedding was most beautifully elaborated in ancient Persia and survived into medieval Persian mysticism.[20] In the Persian tradition, every individual who has been incarnated on earth possesses a guardian angel in heaven (often without knowing it)—his *daena*, a daughter of the cosmic Sophia (Spenta Armaiti).[21] The *daena* is his celestial *alter ego*, his *imago animae*, the mirror of his earthly likeness. *She is formed from his good deeds*, which originate in his active imagination, that is, out of his good thoughts. When a man dies, she appears as a beautiful young girl to meet him at the Chinvat Bridge in the Beyond and accompany him to the other side.[22] She is actually the religious "visionary organ of the soul" itself, "the light it throws and which makes it possible to see."[23] In this sense she is the *religio* of the deceased. She reveals herself to the departed as his own faith, in the sense that it was "she who inspired it in (him), . . . she for whom (he) answered and she who guided (him), who comforted (him) and who now judges (him)."[24] She is also the "image" which he was destined to become; she is glory, victory, and destiny. She is the eternal aspect within mortal man.[25]

This archetypal aspect of the anima of death is also to be found in dreams and visions of contemporary men, for whom the anima is experienced as a demon who takes the dying person away from life or as a welcome beloved who carries him away to a better world. The following dream of a man who died of a sudden heart attack three weeks after the dream is an example of the demon motif. This man was unhappily married, but had tried all his life to maintain his marriage according to conventional Christian standards. He dreamed:

> He was in a church beside his wife—apparently to be married to her again or to reconfirm his marriage. But in front of him was a blank whitewashed wall. The minister was a person whom he knew in reality, a very decent but depressive, neurotic man. Suddenly a most beautiful Gypsy woman broke into the ceremony, fettered the parson with ropes and began to drag him away. At the same time she looked with flaming eyes at the dreamer and said, "And with you, I will soon lose my patience."[26]

As mentioned, the man died shortly after having this dream. His anima was angry because he had not loved her but had entirely suppressed his Eros-nature for the sake of convention. She thus became a death demon, much like the Greek portrayal of death as a birdshaped female being (with a human upper body), the frightful *keres*, who carried the souls of the dead away to Hades.

Frequently, however, the same motif has a more joyful ambiance. Another relatively young man, who died unexpectedly of heart failure while skiing, reported the next to the last dream he had had some weeks before his death:

> At a party of his relatives, he meets a woman and knows immediately that she is *the* woman for him, although he has never encountered her in his outer life. She is very attractive physically, but it is more than that. He feels that she completely embodies the most basic requirements for relationship, that she is independent of him and yet very closely intimate. Wherever she goes, she offers him her hand and obviously

rejoices in his company, but there is no forcing at all in any of this. . . . Together they go to a shop in the city and every moment together is a pure joy.[27]

As Barbara Hannah correctly points out, this encounter with the anima does not necessarily allude to death but, seen after the event, the death-wedding motif is also suggested.[28] This was the case with Socrates, who, in prison, dreamed of a radiantly white woman. He understood the image as an announcement of his death. Such a relation of death to Eros was well-known in ancient Greece. Artemidorus wrote that to dream of a wedding could mean death, for weddings and death "are regarded as turning points in human life and the one always points to the other."[29] Eros, Hypnos (sleep), and Thanatos (death) are brothers who are often interchanged in the iconography, and the grave or tomb is occasionally called *thalamos* (bridal chamber).[30]

A reminiscence of these ancient views may very well have been preserved in the beautiful Rumanian "Mioritza Ballad," in which two envious men plan to slay a handsome young herdsman because the latter is braver than they and richer in flocks of sheep. The herdsman's loyal, clairvoyant lamb warns him of the plan. He then says to the lamb, "Bury me in my earth, together with my belongings, and put different flutes on my grave, through which the wind will play. And say nothing to the flocks that I have been murdered. Tell them:

> *Que j'ai épousé*
> *Reine sans seconde*
> *Promise du monde*
> *Qu'à ces noces là*
> *Un astre fila;*
> *Qu'au dessus du throne*
> *Tenaient ma couronne*
> *La Lune, en atours*
> *Le Soleil, leur cours,*
> *Les grands monts, mes prêtres*
> *Mes témoins, les hêtres*
> *Aux hymnes des voix*
> *Des oiseaux des bois.*
> *Que j'ai eu pour cierges*

> *Les étoiles vierges*
> *Des milliers d'oiseaux*
> *Et d'astres flambeaux.*[31]

This is the death wedding, the union of the soul with the universe, with the *anima mundi* in the womb of nature. The shepherd then requests of the lamb: if his old mother should search for him to tell her only that he has married a queen, but nothing more. He wants to spare her feelings and leave her uncertain as to whether or not he will ever live in this world again. He has returned to the greater mother, to Nature. Most interpreters see in this song a description of a dead man and of his merging with the totality of nature. But it is more accurate to understand it as a marriage with the anima, with the cosmic dimension of the unconscious psyche.

A Ukrainian folk song contains the same motif, albeit in a simpler form. In this song a dying warrior addresses his horse:

> *Neigh out loud!*
> *My old mother comes.*
> *Do not tell her, my steed,*
> *That I lie slain,*
> *Say to her, steed,*
> *That I have wooed*
> *And taken* a little *bride—*
> The grave *in the far clear field.*[32]

And in a Turkish folk-song, the deceased says to his parents:

> *. . . I married yesterday,*
> *Yesterday in the evening very late.*
> *Mother World is my bride;*
> *My mother-in-law the grave.*[33]

As we know, the anima in a man is very closely connected with the mother imago, and this is the reason the bride in the song is also "Mother World"—an *anima mundi* who, for the dead man, is both mother and bride at the same time.

*Fig. 7:* Death-wedding. The sky-goddess Nut lies at the bottom of the coffin, her arms outstretched toward the mummy, with the Ba of the deceased hovering above.

In ancient Greece, as noted above, the innermost coffin chamber of the grave was called *thalamos* (bridal chamber), and the walls of Etruscan tombs were decorated with colorful dionysian scenes of music, dancing, and feasting, as in wedding celebrations. The image-rich Egyptian culture employed the same motif. The lids and bottoms of coffins were frequently painted with representations of Nut, the sky goddess, so that the dead literally rested in her arms; or Isis would be painted on the upper lid and Nepthys underneath. In the "Vigil Hours of Osiris," the mourner in the fifth hour speaks to the deceased:

> Arise my lord (thus speaks your mother Nut); see, I come to protect you, your mother spreads heaven over you in her name. . . . I decorate your body more beautifully than those of the (other) gods. I push your throne over that of the transfigured ones.[34]

For the seventh and eighth hours of the day, the liturgy runs as follows:

> O Osiris, First of the West. Look, your sister Isis comes to you, jubilant with love for you, and she surrounds you with

her protecting magic. Look, your sister Nepthys comes to you.
. . . Isis comes to you. They both protect you.[35]

And in the twelfth hour:

Rise, O Lord! How beautiful are thy limbs; how kind is this
woman to your *ka!* How beautiful is your repose. You, living
one, your female companions embrace you.[36]

And finally, in the tenth hour of the night:

O Osiris, First of the Western Ones, Isis cures you, Nepthys
embraces you. You are the magnificent god among them and
you possess what they do to you.[37]

The nature mysticism of the "Mioritza" song goes back to age-
old ideas which originated in Asia and then spread through all
the eastern Mediterranean basin (Crete, Cyprus, the Cyclades,
the Minoan mainland, etc.). In many of the graves in those
areas, one finds the image of the "great goddess" flanked by
doves, bull, snake, etc. The dead come under their protection
for a renewal of life. In the Middle Bronze Age, as mentioned
above, corpses were often packed in *pithoi* (large storage jars)
where, like seed corn, they awaited resurrection. On Cyprian
vessels one finds the portrayal of a couple, which could very well
represent a dead man and his partner or the *hierosgamos* of a
divine couple. The accompanying doves represent the power of
the great love goddess.[38] The death motif of the *hierosgamos*
belongs psychologically to a world in which the great goddess or
mother goddess and the feminine principle of Eros are predominant. In patriarchal, warrior cultures this motif seems to be
rather less important.

# 4.
# The Dark Birth Passage and the Spirit of Discouragement

*T*he image of a dark, narrow birth passage also belongs among those archetypal motifs which anticipate the course of death. In the Komarios text, the production of gold, or the "stone of the wise," was represented as taking place through a pregnancy and the birth of a child. This is a leitmotif that runs through many centuries of the alchemical tradition.

Similar to the birth image is another motif in the Komarios text: the suggestion that adepts should treat their material like a bird which "hatches its eggs . . . in mild warmth." This idea also occurs over and over again in the the alchemical texts. From the beginning of time, antique man wondered with fascination how an egg, which when opened contains only half-liquid "dead" substances, could still produce a living being, only by being warmed and without the help of any external agent. The alchemists compared the production of their stone to this "miracle."

The *I Ching*, the Chinese oracle book, provides a parallel to this, which seems to me worth mentioning. It concerns the description of a time condition called Chung Fu, "Inner Truth." Richard Wilhelm comments: "The character *fu* ("truth") is actually the picture of a bird's foot over a fledgling. It suggests the idea of brooding. An egg is hollow. The light-giving power must work to quicken it from the outside, but there must be a germ of life within, if life is to be awakened."[1] In a similar manner, and in this case certainly without any cultural transfer, the alchemist Gerhard Dorn (sixteenth century) called the innermost soul, the Self of man, an "inner truth," and he looked upon alchemical work as a "hatching out" of this truth from physical matter.

Birth symbolism is especially and intensively elaborated in the Egyptian death liturgy. Thus in Rubric 170 of the Book of the Dead we read: "Shake off the earth which is in your flesh; you are Horus in his egg."[2] Or, Rubric 85: "I am the Heightened, the Lord of the Ta-Tebu; my name is the Boy in the Place, the Child in the Field."[3] Or: "I am yesterday. My name is He Who

Has Seen Millions of Years. . . . I am the Lord of Eternity. . . .
I am the one in the Udjat Eye, and I am the one in the egg . . .
with it life is given to me."[4] Or: "I enter the world from which I
emerged, after having counted (renewed) my first birth."[5] It is
true that this last rubric concerns the sun god, but every dead
person repeats the fate of the god and, like the sun, is reborn as
child and hatched out as a bird.

To date I have heard only once of such a birth motif in the
dream of a dying person. This was the case of a seventy-four-
year-old woman who died from carcinoma metastases. She had
the dream just two weeks before her death. She had been very ill
the day before, yet she made much seemingly futile effort to
bring some order into her outer affairs. As a result, she developed painful stomach cramps, after which she dreamed:

> She was lying across the opening of a cement pipe about one
> meter wide, whose upper edge pressed painfully against her
> stomach. The pipe itself was stuck into the earth. She knew
> that she had to emerge from it headfirst and intact into another
> land.

Upon awakening, her association for the "other land" was a
"land of dwarfs and spirits" of which she had previously
dreamed.

The later dream seems to me to express the following: The
pipe appears as a birth passage into another existence. The
dreamer was supposed to go through it headfirst, like an infant
when it is being born. For the moment, however, she lies across
it, because she is still engaged with the concerns of this world
and resists the dark passage. The land into which she is supposed to be born is the "land of dwarfs and spirits"—psychological language for the collective unconscious, which indeed has
always been and still is "under" our world of consciousness, even
when we do not notice it.

The physicians Raymond Moody[6] and Michael Sabom[7] and
the theologian Johann Christoph Hampe[8] report similar "passage" motifs in their respective works.[9] They deal with cases of
heart failure, after which the patients were "brought back to life"
artificially. Most of these patients describe their experience as

one of being in a very happy state, but quite often some of them had first to go through something resembling a short blackout[10] or through a dark valley or tunnel before they could arrive at a new state of existence. A clinically dead woman who was reanimated by means of an adrenalin injection described her experience in the following terms:

> I was floating in a long tunnel, which at first seemed quite narrow, then became wider and wider. It was dark red over me and blue-black in front of me. However, the higher I looked the brighter it became. The feeling of weightlessness was wonderful.[11]

Another case:

> I found myself again inside a dark spiral-shaped tunnel. At the far end of the tunnel, which was very narrow, I saw a bright light.[12]

When obliged to return to life by medical treatment, some of these patients reported that they had to come back through the same tunnel by which they departed.

One can also dream of the death of *another* person as a departure through such an obstacle. Thus a woman dreamed the following before the death of her father:

> I am in an underground station and I suddenly discover my father among the people waiting for a train. He does not seem to notice me but walks on ahead. He is wearing a dark blue suit and looks very well, a bit thinner than before. I follow him, but the great distance between us always remains the same, whether I go faster or slower. He is not to be reached. Suddenly I see him disappear in front of a bright wall at the end of the tunnel. He walks through the wall and where he had been there appear small things that are difficult for me to recognize from the distance. Then I meet my mother. She says that she saw father disappear and that many rabbits fell out of the wall at that spot. I tell her that rabbits are a symbol of fertility and that I find it meaningful that death, too, is still fertile.

The dream speaks for itself. The rabbits indicate that the father's death will bring the dreamer psychological growth in her own life.

Death is described in dreams sometimes not as a tunnel passage but as a heavy dark spot which spreads out and hangs over the dreamer, or as a cloud which completely obliterates all view of the outer world. The last dream of the dying woman whose case David Eldred has given us in his dissertation contains the motif of a resistance to this darkness, for she had to exert a great effort not to fall into a calm, deep mountain lake.[13] This probably also characterizes the fear of "blackout" at the moment of death or, perhaps still deeper, a fear of becoming unconscious, together with a loss of ego identity.[14]

A young woman suffering from an incurable disease, who died unexpectedly during a surgical operation, dreamed, before the lethal intervention:

> I find myself at the edge of a lake with my husband and some friends. The lake is very deep and the water is clear, transparent, clean and blue. Suddenly I see a black bird in the depths of the lake; it is dead. I feel great sympathy and want to dive in, search for it and save it. I cannot stand to think that it is dead. My husband intervenes lovingly but firmly and asks me not to do it, because, he says, it is right this way. I look into the lake once more and see the eye of the bird; it is a diamond that shines brightly. Whereupon I awaken.

The dead bird must be the extinguished life spirit of the body which the dreamer must abandon, otherwise she would be contaminated with the dissolving powers of death. She must keep herself free of the dying body, but at the same time she looks at the diamond eye of the bird. The diamond (from *adamas*, "invincible") is an alchemical variant of the Self as an indestructible core of personality.

The woman whose active imagination, given earlier, centered around a flower reported the following dream, the last before her death:

> She had a black spot in her eye. If it should ever reach the center of the eye, she would feel a short acute pain, but Mrs. X would help her to endure it.

This black spot—as later became evident—was death, which "darkens" the eyes, that is, puts an end forever to all sight of the outer world. Mrs. X was a woman for whom the dreamer had great respect and who had a greater psychological knowledge than the dreamer, so that in this case she stands for the Self, which helps her through the painful passage.

We frequently find indefinite darkness as a death image in the literature of antiquity. The Greek *thanatos* ("death") was often imagined as a *dark* black or purple-red cloud, or as a patch of fog which darkens the eyes.[15] (*Thanatos* is more impersonal than the so-called *keres*, those fateful personal death demons that carried away the dying person.) *Thanatos* rarely appears personified; if so, then as a serious, bearded, winged man who takes the dying into his arms in a not-unfriendly manner.

The dark spot as a death motif appears in a dream, reported by Mark Pelgrin, of a woman who died shortly afterward:

> As I seem to awaken, I see a coloured circle which is thrown on the screen of the curtain that hangs down in front of the window in our bedroom. . . . I am walking gingerly around this circle which seems to be black, as though I must tread carefully or I will fall in. This is evidently a pit, the black hole.[16]

The circle is an image of the Self; in the dream it is colored, that is, full of life, but appears black when the dreamer comes close to it, like a black hole which she would anxiously like to avoid. Paradoxically enough, in coming close to the Self there emanates from it an attraction to it and, at the same time, a fear of it. The fear of death is thereby in the last analysis a fear of the Self and of the final inner confrontation with the Self.

The dream of an individual who died a few days afterward was reported as follows:

> In the middle of a picture I see a black square. It is a kind of medieval night chest. Flashes of red light stream from it. These flashes point to a sky, painted in pastel colors, mostly yellow and blue, with a radiant sun (on the upper right side of the picture).

The night chest is reminiscent of a coffin, the place of one's final sleep. But out of it come flashes of light, that is, symbols of sudden illumination, pointing to a pale blue sky—a common image of the Beyond—and to the sun, a symbol of the cosmic source of the light of consciousness. The flashes also remind us of Origen's concept of resurrection as a *spintherismos*, an emission of sparks from the corpse, the departure of the soul from the dead body. In Islamic tradition, the deceased must cross over the so-called Sirat Bridge, "thinner than a hair, sharper than a sword and darker than the night," but the pious "get there quickly like a flash of lightning."[17] The night chest in the above dream seems to me to be a variant of the dark passage.

The dark passage is frequently depicted directly and concretely in the architecture of tombs. Emily Vermeule reports that Mycenean graves represent a model for the general geography of the land of the dead (Hades). There is first a downward passage (*dromos*), then a narrow gap (*stomion*, "mouth"), and then the high, wide grave chamber (*thalamos*, "bridal chamber").[18] The grave chamber itself is like a womb in the earth, which the dead enter to await rebirth.

Shaft graves, found in many excavation areas, may be closely connected with the symbol of the dark birth passage. This symbol, which essentially points to a purely *psychic experience* of a temporary confinement, of fear, of blackout, is thus mixed in an archaic way with the idea of the concrete grave or coffin.[19]

In ancient Egypt the grave was also designed as a cave, in which a process of rebirth occurs in the ground water. The shaft tunnel of a king's grave was described as "a cave of Sokar," the mythical place of the rejuvenation and rebirth of the dead.[20] In many parts of Africa corpses are still buried in a crouching or embryonic position. With the Zulus, for instance, the widow of the dead man receives his body on her lap in the grave, then puts it into a niche which is called the "navel." She places seeds in his hands (!), which will prepare the deceased for rebirth. After some time the dead body is brought back to the village as the "spirit of the ancestors,"[21] where it bestows fertility and protection onto the living.

The Hopi Indians of North America believe that the soul of the deceased goes through a small square cavity, the so-called Sipàpu, which leads to the Kiwa buildings. This cavity has the connotation of a sacred place and is regarded as the place of origin, that opening through which the Hopi tribe came up from the depths to the surface of the world.[22]

The "dark birth event" as *psychic* experience is described in the Komarios text, to which we now return.

> Observe the mystery of the philosophers; on behalf of this mystery our forefathers have sworn not to reveal it or to propagate it, for it has a divine form and a divine effect. It is divine because—having become one with the deity—it perfects the substance whereby the spirits are incarnated and the dead person is reanimated and receives (again) the spirit (*pneuma*) which had issued from it, and is conquered thereby, and they (spirit and body) conquer each other. For the dark spirit (is) so full of futility (*mataiotes*) and discouragement (*athymias*) that the bodies cannot become white and cannot receive the beauty and the color which they have obtained from the creator (for body, soul and spirit are weakened because of the spread-out darkness).[23]

The initial darkness in the Beyond (Hades) is here called the spirit of futility (*mataiotes*) and the spirit of discouragement (*athymias*). This is a condition of very deep depression and a feeling of complete meaninglessness.[24] *Thanatos*, "death," is often referred to in ancient Greece as *thymoraistes*, "he who strikes down the *thymos*." *Thymos* is the courage to face life or the life impulse. Kübler-Ross has described this depression in many cases of dying people, in whom it appears, of course, before the actual end.[25] In my opinion, it serves to help detach the consciousness of the dying person from the outer world; the latter is experienced in the depression as more or less meaningless, futile, unreal. In the above dream, it is the eyes which are affected by the dark fog, as they are to be understood as symbolizing one's view of the outer world, which must now be terminated in favor of a complete about-face toward the *inner* images. The spirit of discouragement is related to the fact that the ego still looks too much toward the outside, at the visible world, and does not yet sufficiently see the "reality of the soul." Christa Meves reports the dream of a totally irreligious woman, who was committed to a rationalistic-materialistic attitude toward the world. Her dream makes very clear this spirit of meaninglessness.

> I am standing, quite confused, inside a courtyard. There is no exit. On one side of the yard are garbagemen who say that I cannot get out of the yard because it is a machine for demolishing cars. Another man thinks that there is a revolving door through which he could get me out. But I am afraid that it might be a trap, so I remain in the yard and walk in circles along the walls. I behave like the others, like a pedestrian, but inside I am tortured by the fear of not being able to find my home.[26]

Since this woman consciously recognized no inner, spiritual values, she remained identical with her body. But as the dream reports, in rough language, the body goes to a garbage dump. (In present-day dreams a car often symbolizes the body, or our customary way of moving around in the outer world.) The dreamer is afraid of going through the revolving door, which, in this instance, replaces the otherwise usual tunnel passage. Characteristically enough, it is a *revolving* door; if she tried to go through it, it would revolve around a center, about 180 degrees. A *turn-around* would therefore come about if she would only summon up enough trust to follow the man who offers her help. But she thinks it is a trap; that is, she thinks, like so many people, that religious traditions are only "opium for the people" or wish-fulfillment dreams. As a result, she remains a slave to the spirit of futility and goes around on one spot in an unfortunate vicious circle. This gloomy image reminds one of some of the experiences reported by Moody, in which his witnesses are said to have spent some time in a kind of "in-between" region where shadowy spirits of the dead wandered about mindlessly.[27]

> What you would think of as their head was bent downward; they had sad, depressed looks; they seemed to shuffle. . . . They looked washed out, dull, grey. And they seemed to be forever shuffling and moving around, not knowing where they were going, not knowing who to follow, or what to look for. . . . They seemed to be . . . very bewildered; not knowing who they are or what they are. It looks like they have lost any knowledge of who they are, what they are—no identity whatsoever.[28]

This gloomy picture of life after death agrees—much more than do those "experiences of light" also described by Moody[26]

—with the numerous stories from all over the world of haunt-
ings, of ghosts, and of the spirits of the dead. In our experience
of dreams, too, the Beyond of the unconscious is very seldom
represented by beautiful images. Equally often, dreams present
oppressive scenes. What seems to be decisive is how psychologically mature a person is before death and whether or not he or
she has developed a relationship with the Self.

This turnaround is consolingly described in a dream of an
old woman reported by Dr. Jay Dunn: [29]

> She sees a candle lit on the window sill of the hospital room
> and finds that the candle suddenly goes out. Fear and anxiety
> ensue as the darkness envelops her. Suddenly, the candle lights
> on the other side of the window and she awakens. [30]

The patient died the same day, completely at peace. The dream
passage here contains an element of momentary fear and anxiety.
Somehow the candle gets through the closed window to the
other side, as if it had dematerialized and then materialized again
in another place. The moment of depression and fear is quite
short in this instance; in some dreams it lasts much longer.

The dark passage is represented in other dreams as a journey to the West, to the place of the setting sun. Not only in the
widespread custom of shipboard burial, in which the corpse is
sent out to sea in a boat, is death conceived as a journey to an
unknown land, generally situated in the West. [31] In my experience the image of the journey in dreams is also the most frequently occurring symbol of impending death. It is so frequent
in fact that it will not be dealt with to any great extent here.

An old woman, for instance, dreamed shortly before her
death:

> I have packed two suitcases, one with my working clothes, the
> other, a trans-Europe suitcase, with my jewelry, my diaries
> and my photos. The first is for the mainland, the other for
> America. [32]

Over there (in the Westland) she may not be able to take along
her everyday attitude (her working clothes) but she can take her
inner psychic treasures.

*Fig. 8:* Sunrise, as represented on a *djed* pillar (with the heiroglyph for "duration" and an image of Osiris). For the Egyptians the sun symbolized the highest form of consciousness, the sunrise representing, at the same time, resurrection.

This motif also appears in a case reported by Whitmont of a woman who was doomed to die. She dreamed:

I met my husband, who told me that everything would be all right and that I need not worry. I then bade him goodbye and found myself at the seashore. The beach was lonely and the light was darkening; the shore was empty except for some barges.[33]

We find the motif of the journey most extensively, however, in the Egyptian cult of the dead, where the *bau* [34] souls of the blessed complete their journey with the sun god in his bark. The journey to the Beyond follows the path of the sun. It begins with a descent into the underworld, into the "cave of Sokar," and leads, through various obstructed areas, to the East, where the deceased, together with the sun god, returns to life, rejuvenated. He then leaves his mummy behind in the underworld and in his *ba* form accompanies the sun god, who has been reborn in the East. The sun, as the goal of the pathway of the dead, also appeared in the above dream of the black night chest. It symbolizes the highest awareness as the goal of the individuation process. The directional burial orientation of numerous ancient and still existing cultures also points to this idea, namely that resurrection is at the same time something like a new sunrise.

This comparison of the sun's path with the mystery of life and death has had an especially rich development in Egypt. The sun, for the Egyptians, was the guarantor of all order. "Night, darkness and death are therefore dangerous for man because they have to do with the world before and outside creation, and that means outside of order. In this non-order, which the Egyptian bluntly calls nonbeing, human life is not possible, as it is not possible without the sun." [35] Thus, it was finally the sun, "which, as a symbol of the new life after death, the Egyptians served with the utmost seriousness and with enormous material and intellectual expenditure." [36]

Seen psychologically then, the sun is a symbol of the source of *awareness*.

The cosmic significance of becoming conscious, one might say, became apparent to Jung during his travels in Africa.

> At that time I understood that within the soul from its primordial beginnings there has been a desire for light and an irrepressible urge to rise out of the primal darkness. When the great night comes, everything takes on a note of deep dejection, and every soul is seized by an inexpressible longing for light. That is the pent-up feeling that can be detected in the eyes of primitives, and also in the eyes of animals. There is a sadness in animals' eyes, and we never know whether that sadness is bound up with the soul of the animal or is a poignant message which speaks to us out of that still unconscious existence. That sadness also reflects the mood of Africa, the experience of its solitudes. It is a maternal mystery, this primordial darkness. That is why the sun's birth in the morning strikes the natives as so overwhelmingly meaningful. The *moment* in which light comes *is* God. That moment brings redemption, release. To say that the *sun* is God is to blur and forget the archetypal

experience of that moment. "We are glad that the night when the spirits are abroad is over now," the natives will say—but that is already a rationalization. In reality a darkness altogether different from natural night broods over the land. It is the psychic primal night which is the same today as it has been for countless millions of years. The longing for light is the longing for consciousness.[37]

For the Egyptian, participation in the life of the sun meant, therefore, participation also in the increasing process of becoming conscious and of the evolving culture of man.

This meaning of light also lies behind the widespread custom of lighting candles (in antiquity, torches) and letting them burn in mortuary rooms and on tombs and graves. This is a form of analogy magic,[38] through which new life and an awakening to new consciousness is granted to the deceased.

# 5.
# Death as the Sinister
# or Benevolent Other

*T*he nearness of death is frequently represented in dreams by the image of a burglar, that is, by someone unfamiliar which unexpectedly enters one's present life. A businessman in his middle fifties wanted to undergo analysis with me, for he felt frustrated in his work and was looking for a deeper meaning in life. His first dream:

> He awakens in the middle of the night in bed, in a dark room halfway under the earth. A bright gleam of light streams in through the window. Suddenly he sees a stranger in the room, someone who fills him with such an inhuman, terrible fear that he awakens, bathed in sweat.

The first dream in an analysis is often prophetic; it anticipates future developments which are being prepared, as it were, in the unconscious. I did not understand this man's dream and confined myself to the remark that something that is still very strange and fearful wants to come to him and that it would have some connection with light, that is, with illumination, with insight. After a couple of analytic hours the dreamer never showed up again; from time to time, however, he assured me by telephone that he wanted very much to continue the analysis but that he was overburdened with work. A year later I heard that he was about to die from cancer of the spinal cord. The sinister "intruder" of the initial dream had been clearly death itself.

R. Lindner reports a similar dream from a man who died soon thereafter:

> I come home and close the apartment door. As I enter, I have the feeling that something is there. . . . I look into my room and see an old man over sixty whom I have observed occasionally on the tram; he looks like death. He has come into the house as a burglar. Horrified, I run out of the house but I cannot lock the door from the outside so I knock at a neighbor's door and call for help. But there is no one to be seen there and

no one opens the door for me. I am all alone. I go back to my apartment where the sinister man is still in my room.[1]

The previously mentioned patient of Edinger's experienced his first death premonition in a similar way. Six months before he died he dreamed:

I am at home but it's nowhere I've been before. I go into the pantry to get some food. The shelves are stacked with seasonings and spices, all the same brand, but there is nothing to eat. I feel I am not alone in the house. It is just turning dawn or is it the brilliant moonlight? I turn on the light but it comes from another room. Something creaks. I am not alone. I wonder where my dog is. I need more light. I need more light and more courage. I am afraid.[2]

This invisible presence of a sinister "other" also refers to death.

Kurt Lückel reports a similar dream of a seventy-eight-year-old woman:

I hear someone knocking at the front door, then at an inside door. After that, someone enters my room, stops by the door and waits. I cannot tell whether it is a man or a woman. He (!) stands by the door but does not come closer, just stands there and waits. I get scared. I have an uncanny feeling. I shout at him: "What do you want from me? Don't ever come back here again!" . . . But I am unable to go back to sleep.[3]

In discussing the dream she realized herself that this intruder could have been "a messenger of God," that is, death.

In the mythologies of many cultures death appears either as a male or female figure. Edgar Herzog has given us an impressive picture of the mythically personified figures of death and has shown that the names of the Germanic goddess Hel and of the Greek nymph Calypso have the same origin, from the Indo-Germanic verbal stem *kel(u)*, meaning "to hide in the earth."[4] Certain primitive Asiatic peoples know a demon (sometimes with a dog's face) called Kala, plural Kalau, who personifies death and illness.[5]

Death is more often represented as a wolf or dog, however, than as a sinister "other" in human form. Hel, for instance, is the sister of the Fenris wolf, the latter corresponding to the Greek Cerberus, son of the Echidna serpent.[6] Popular beliefs of the Germans and Swiss have preserved legends in which the appearance of a black dog announces death. The night Jung's mother died, an event of which he was not yet aware, he dreamed:

> I was in a dense, gloomy forest. . . . It was a heroic, primeval landscape. Suddenly I heard a piercing whistle. . . . My knees shook. Then there were crashings in the underbrush, and a gigantic wolfhound with a fearful, gaping maw burst forth. . . . It tore past me, and I suddenly knew: the Wild Huntsman had commanded it to carry away a human soul. . . . The next morning I received the news of my mother's passing.[7]

The Wild Huntsman, Jung explains, is Wotan, the Mercury of the alchemists. Thus the dream clearly says that the soul of his mother "was taken into that greater territory of the self . . . into that wholeness of nature and spirit in which conflicts and contradictions are resolved."[8] The dog is also often described mythologically as a healing and protecting escort into the Beyond.[9] Thus the Egyptian dog-headed or jackal-headed god Anubis is the agent of resurrection; and among the Aztecs a yellow or red dog, Xolotl, brings the corpses in the kingdom of the dead back to life. In India, too, Shiva, the destroying god of death, is called Lord of the Dogs. The Batavian death-goddess Nehalennia was portrayed with a basket of apples (the fruits!) on one side and a wolfhound on the other.[10] And Vergil tells us in the *Aeneid* that the hell-dog Cerberus is actually the earth which devours corpses. Snakes and birds can also, on occasion, represent death.

In an impressive paper in which she interprets death experiences psychologically,[11] Liliane Frey reports an interesting case in which the "other" appears as the *devil*. The dreamer was a healthy, successful young man who had the following dream during a trip to the Near East:

> I flew with a young boy up the steep slope of a meadow. Before reaching the plain above us . . . the devil appeared on the scene, from the left. He noticed me, came close to me and said that he would soon have to deal with me. I stood there, half-

respectful, half-arrogant, and said, "I know this much, if that time will only come, I will get away alive." The devil laughed and said that there would still be some scattered pleasures. His face was dark brown and he wore a long dark Arabian shirt; when he straightened the garment every possible color appeared in its folds. There was a cinnamon-red spot on one of his cheeks. It looked to me like a brand, like the black spider.[12]

A few days later the dreamer died in an airplane accident in the Arabian desert. The "black spider,"[13] as he himself wrote, indicates the "Great Mother." Thus, as Frey explains, he actually succumbed to the superior force of the unconscious, that is, to his connection with the Great Mother. If we amplify this dream a bit further, then this devil, dressed as an Arab, reminds one of certain Arabic alchemical traditions in which the "stone of the wise," the Self, appears first as a murderous enemy of the adept. In the Arabic "Book of Ostanes," for instance, it is said of the stone of the wise that it is

> a tree that grows on the tops of the mountains [!], a young man born in Egypt, a prince from Andalusia who desires the torment of the seekers. He has slain their leaders. . . . The sages are powerless to oppose him. I can see no weapon against him save resignation, no charger but knowledge, no buckler but understanding. If the seeker finds himself before him with these three weapons, and slays him, he (the prince) will come to life again after his death, will lose all power against him, and will give the seeker the highest power, so that he will arrive at his desired goal.[14]

Jung elucidates this passage by referring first to Enkidu, the chthonic opponent of the Sumerian hero Gilgamesh, who appears at the beginning of the epic as an enemy, then after his victory over Gilgamesh is transformed into a friend. "Psychologically, this means that at the first meeting with the self all those negative qualities can appear which almost invariably characterize an unexpected encounter with the unconscious."[15]

Another alchemical text also speaks of the stone of the wise: "This stone proceeds from a sublime and most glorious place of great terror, which has given over many sages to death."[16] The sinister "other," whom I have interpreted in the above dreams as death, is therefore nothing other than the Self. Death and Self—God's image, that is—are *de facto* indistinguishable.

In the dream of Frey's patient, the colors shining from the folds of the devil's garment reveal that this devil figure is, in fact, a Mercury figure, for in the alchemical texts it is often said of the spirit Mercury that he wears *omnes colores*, "all colors." The iridescence *(cauda pavonis)* appears in the alchemical process after the *nigredo* (blackening), as is indicated here by the "devil" who still provides "some scattered pleasures"—this means that there will still be life after passing through the *nigredo*.

The death god Yama, "all in black, tall, robust," or sometimes one of his messengers, the so-called Yamdus, appears frequently to dying East Indian patients in order to take them into the Beyond.[17] Patients who have grown up in the Christian tradition often see angels in the same role.[18] From the psychological point of view, the sinister burglar generally appears more often as an image of the personal "other" half of the soul of the dying individual, whereas in the figures of Hermes, devil, Yama, angel, we encounter something closer to a symbol of the Self in its suprapersonal aspect. Seen psychologically, these aspects merge and overlap, and they are often, in a culture-specific sense, very differently described.

From my own experience, it seems to me that the terror-filled, uncanny aspect of the "other" appears especially when the dreamer has as yet *no relation to death or does not expect it*. Basically, the figures of personified death (death, devil, Yama, Jesus, Hades, Hel, etc.) seem to be nothing other than *a dark side of the god image*. It is actually God, or a goddess, who brings death to man and the less familiar he is with this dark side of the divine the more negative his experience of it will be. But the great religions have always known that death and life are a part of the same divine mystery which lies behind man's physical existence.

Personified death, or that "other" who comes to take away the living, sometimes also appears in dreams as an explicit positive figure.[19] Thus an analysand of mine who was in his middle fifties had the following initial dream:

> He walked in a field, it was a gloomy atmosphere, the sky was clouded over. Suddenly a slit opened between the clouds and,

in a ray of sunshine, the shape of a beautiful naked youth was looking down on him. He felt an indescribable feeling of love and happiness.

This dream frightened me because I thought at once of Hermes, the guide of souls, coming for and leading the dead into the Beyond. As it soon became clear, the health of this man had been ruined during the war and the analysis became an urgent preparation for his early death. Hermes is the interpreter and ruler of dreams, the mediator in any contact with the contents of the unconscious;[20] but on Etruscan inscriptions he is also called *turmaitas*, "the Hermes of Hades"!

As this man lay dying in the hospital he kept muttering all the while to himself (as a friend later reported to me): "What does this beautiful Indian woman want from me?" Here the figure of the guide had obviously become the anima,[21] as in the previously mentioned dream. For a European "Indian" means exotic, mysterious, difficult to understand. A still unknown aspect of his own soul comes to the dying man in order to conduct him to the other side. Whether this figure is male or female, anima (with a woman, animus) or Self, does not in itself seem to be important. In each case it has something to do with a personification of the still unknown unconscious. That is why in mythologies the world over, death appears as male or as female. As mentioned before, the ancient Persians believed that in the Beyond the dying person must first cross over the Chinvat Bridge. For an evil person the bridge is only as wide as a hair and, as a result, he falls down into the world of demons. A young boy, or more frequently a fifteen-year-old girl, comes to meet the pious person, however, and helps him across. Henri Corbin has thoroughly elucidated the meaning of this figure.[22] She is identical with the Persian *xvarnah*—a word which means something like a personal "radiance" or "fate." The *xvarnah* is also the "visionary organ of the soul," the light that makes seeing possible and that itself is seen, the vision of the heavenly world that has been lived as religion and as faith and with it the essential individuality, the transcendental earthly "ego." She is also the "image" which was formed before the dying individual, before his birth, and the "image" which later in life he will eventually desire. She is his lifetime (his *aion*) and the eternity of every man. If the departed has betrayed this "image," he falls from the Chinvat Bridge into the Abyss of the demons.[23]

Similar ideas are also to be found in Manichaeism. Mani himself received his revelations through an angel of the *al taum* (twin), therefore his *doppelgänger*, who was the mediator, the paraclete.[24] According to his teaching, the soul of every dead man gets a look at the image of its "master." "As soon as the soul has left the body, it catches sight of its savior and redeemer. She ascends, together with the image of her master and the three angels with him, and proceeds to the Judges of Truth and receives the victory."[25] The "mediator is a light figure, an outer image of the cosmic spirit. The soul then enters the 'bridal chamber' of the Light."[26]

This companion *doppelgänger*, or image of the Self, can be experienced, in mystical ecstasy, when one is still alive. The Islamic mystic Ibn 'Arabi, for instance, saw him in a vision as a handsome youth, "the Silent Speaker, him who is neither living nor dead, the composite-simple, the enveloped-enveloping."[27] He beheld the youth as the latter was being transformed into the Ka'aba, and he understood him, more or less, as the soul of the sacred stone. While the conventional believer sees in the Ka'aba only a "solid mineral with no life," Ibn 'Arabi beheld its actual essence "with the eyes of the heart." The youth he saw spoke only in symbols.[28] He said to the visionary:

> "Note well the articulations of my nature, the ordering of my structure. What you ask me you will find in myself, for I am not someone who speaks words or to whom words are spoken. My knowledge extends only to myself, and my essence (my person) is no other than my Names. I am Knowledge, the Known and the Knower. I am Wisdom, the work of wisdom and the Sage.[29] . . . I am the Garden of ripe fruit, I am the fruit of the totality. Raise now my veils and read everything that is disclosed in the lines graven on my being."[30]

In a more naive form, we find the same archetypal image of the Self in the experiences, related by Moody, Hampe, and Sabom, of people who were briefly "dead" clinically and were then "brought back to life" through heart massage. The reports of many such patients emphasize having encountered a light or a "light being." A woman, a witness of Moody, formulated this meeting in the following way:

> I floated right . . . up into this pure crystal clear light, an illuminating white light. It was beautiful and so bright, so radiant. . . . It's not any kind of light you can describe on earth. I didn't actually see a person in this light, and yet it has a special identity, it definitely does. It is a light of perfect understanding and perfect love.[31]

Another witness reported:

> I turned over and tried to get into a more comfortable position, but just at that moment a light appeared in the corner of the room, just below the ceiling. It was just a ball of light, almost like a globe, and it was not very large, I would say no more than twelve to fifteen inches in diameter, and as this light appeared, a feeling came over me. I can't say that it was an eerie feeling, because it was not. It was a feeling of complete peace and utter relaxation. I could see a hand reach down for me from the light, and the light said, "Come with me. I want to show you something." So immediately, without any hesitation whatsoever, I reached up with my hand and grabbed onto the hand I saw. As I did, I had the feeling of being drawn up and of leaving my body, and I looked back and saw it lying there on the bed while I was going up towards the ceiling of the room.
>
> Now, at this time, as soon as I left my body, I took on the same form of light. . . . It wasn't a body, just a wisp of smoke or a vapor. . . . The form I took had colors though. There was orange, yellow, and a color that was very indistinct to me—I took it to be an indigo, a bluish color.
>
> This spiritual form didn't have a shape like a body. It was more or less circular, but it had what I would call a hand.[32]

What is most important in this report is that the experiencing person becomes assimilated to this figure of light, and I will return to this detail later. For the present, however, I would like to consider the figure of the light being. Some of Moody's witnesses call it Christ or an angel. In the language of Jungian psychology, it is a visual form of the Self. The latter appears as a source of discrimination, something which, through its heightened intensity, extinguishes normal body consciousness.

The previously mentioned experiences of light are often also accompanied by a psychic illumination, a kind of instruction for the dying person. Thus, one individual cited by Hampe describes:

> "I found myself once again in the darkness, in the inside of a spiral-shaped tunnel. At the far end of the tunnel, which was very narrow, I saw a bright light. Then someone began to talk to me. Someone was there in the darkness. He began by explaining to me the meaning of my life. Every question which anyone could possibly ask was answered for me." Then the voice ordered her to return to life, for her time had not yet come.[33]

An analysand who died in his sixties from a lung disease told his son the following dream which he had had in the hospital and which was his last dream:

> He was leaving the hospital and walking toward an old gate, which in the Middle Ages was the exit from the city. There he met Jung, who was dead and had become the king of the realm of the dead. Jung said to him: "Now, you must make up your mind if you want to go on living and continue your work [he was a painter] or if you want to leave your body." Then the dreamer saw that his sickbed in the hospital was also his easel.

Forty-eight hours after this dream the man died peacefully. The dream seems to me to tell us that it is important to meet death *consciously*, that one should make up one's mind about it, so to speak. That the sickbed is identical with the easel would indicate that now the dreamer has to concentrate his creative efforts on dying, just as he had concentrated them before on his painting. The instructing companion here is Jung, for whom the dreamer had great respect and upon whom he projected the image of the Self.

This "other" (whether male or female) who comes for the dying person is most frequently represented by a dead relative (often the mother), or a marriage partner, or by a recently deceased acquaintance. There are so many examples of this phenomenon that spiritualists have been led to believe that the dead come to fetch the dying and assist them in their adjustment to the after-death condition. Therefore, I will limit myself here to mentioning only a very few examples which appear to me especially authentic.

Thus a woman dreamed that her dead sister, who had died young, was smiling radiantly, holding in her hands a snow-white mourning wreath. The following day she received news of the accidental death of the sister's ten-year-old godchild.[34] Another witness reported a dream in which her long-dead sister appeared, dressed in white, and said to her: "I've come for mother." Exactly two months later the mother died.[35]

Visions do not differ from such dreams. In them, too, dead relatives, marriage partners or friends often come to fetch the dying person. Emil Mattiesen has assembled a great number of examples which contain the motif of "being fetched" by relatives and close friends; therefore I will dispense with further examples here.

# 6.
# The Passage through Fire and Water

*W*e may now return to the Komarios text and focus our attention on the one motif which was often stressed in previously cited passages but not yet interpreted, namely, that the substances are "tested" in fire, and that a child or an immortal one is born "out of the womb of the fire." This motif also appears in the death dreams of contemporary men and women, as for instance in the dream of the doctor in which a coffin was put into a fire and from which a beautiful woman then emerged.

The analysand whose dream of the upper and lower forests was cited had a subsequent dream in which the fire motif appeared. After the consoling dream, which said that life would continue in the upper forest, he was indeed more peacefully prepared for death, but he could not rid himself of a certain bitterness that he must die so relatively young (at the age of fifty-two), "for there are so many things I still want to do in this life," as he remarked. He then dreamed:

> He saw a wood which was green, not yet autumnal. A fire was raging, which destroyed it completely. It was a terrible sight. Afterwards, he was walking through the burned-up area. Everything was turned into black coal and ashes, but in the midst lay a big round boulder of red stone. It showed no trace of the fire, and the dreamer thought: That one the fire has not touched or even blackened!

This dream describes a devastating fire which destroys all "vegetative life." One can understand it as symbolizing the body's destruction by the wildly proliferating cancer, but it can also be seen as an indication that the dreamer's psychic intensity (fire usually means this in most dreams) has become so strong that it destroys the life of the body. This reminds us of the motif of the world-fire, which, according to Simon Magus, destroys the visible parts of the world tree—everything except its "fruit," the soul.

In an important essay, "Cancer in Myth and Dream," Russell Lockhart reports the dream of a patient diseased with cancer:

> I am in a field . . . and I see some men. . . . They are wearing grotesque masks which make them look very tall. . . . They shoot some trees with fire and the leaves immediately burn up and then the fire goes out . . . but the trees look burnt. . . . They take off their masks. . . . They have business suits on and they are satisfied with what they have done. . . . I can see helicopters in the distance shooting something that I know will kill the fruit on the trees.[1]

Here, too, the fire has reference to the destruction of vegetative life. But it has an additional meaning. In Greek alchemy the psyche is frequently said to be *kaustike*, "burning." For instance, the alchemist Zosimos says: "From the beginning one calls the psyche divine and burning nature." Or: "Psyche means the primordially burning divine nature; the spirit *(pneuma)* operates together with it and saves and cleanses it through the fire, if it is skillfully guarded. That is to say, it cannot be ruined."[2] The quotation of Maria Prophetissa also mentions this substance frequently: "Do not touch it (the mystery substance) with the hand, for it is a fiery elixir *(pharmakon)*. . . . It brings death when it decays as quicksilver; the decomposing gold that is in it is extremely pernicious."[3] Or:

> The whitening is an incineration. The burning, however, is at the same time a reanimation through fire. The substances in themselves burn each other and bring themselves back to life through fire and they impregnate each other, making each other pregnant and bringing forth the life being sought after by the philosophers.[4]

Such alchemical amplifications describe a burning process which is simultaneously identical with a fiery reanimation of the dead (the so-called *anazopyresis*). The forest fire in the above dream can also be understood in this sense; a fire destroys all vegetation, but when it is over something indestructible remains, the red stone which was not even blackened by the fire. This stone is such a familiar symbol of the goal in alchemy that I can refer to the sources without citing each of them individually. In the Greek texts it is explicitly stated of the end result that, among other things, the stone of the wise, the lapis, is *pyrimachos*, "able to withstand the fire." Thus, for instance, Zosimos says:

> In this way the spirits are incarnated and the corpses reanimated, in that their souls are sorted out for them again and they complete the divine work; they conquer each other and are conquered by each other. The fleeing pneuma meets together with the pursuing body, when the latter has learned to resist the fire.[5]

Seen, then, in the light of alchemical tradition, the red stone in the dream of the cancer patient would be nothing less than a vision of the resurrection body (or the *lapis qui resistit igni*). This explains why the dreamer felt such an intense satisfaction when he realized that the stone had not even been blackened, that is, it remained quite untouched by the fire.

J. C. Hampe reports an experience of the Beyond by a dying man who wanders with his father through a magnificent landscape:

> I found a large stone and turned it over; it was weightless. On the back of it there was a large number of the most beautiful mountain crystals. They were arranged together to form something resembling a cathedral. I felt happy about it.[6]

This "stone" always seems to be of importance to the experiencing subject, but how it fits into the whole death experience is still obscure for the moment. I will therefore return to this question later.

In the Christian tradition, the realm of the dead, as we know, is described as "fiery," that is, as hellfire and as purgatory fire. The idea of purgatory fire was not generally established as part of the Catholic teaching about the Beyond until the twelfth century.[7] But we do find in the Early Church Fathers some indefinite ideas concerning the sojourn of souls in an intermediary realm before the Final Judgment. Orphic-Pythagorian, Platonic, and especially Egyptian images have exerted not a small influence on these concepts, whereas the Old Testament's Sheol, a dark loamy place, does not play a large role. A fiery Beyond *is* mentioned in the Book of Henoch (second-first century B.C.) which points to Egyptian influences.[8] And in the Apocalypse of Esdras[9] the Beyond—in contradistinction to Paradise—is called the Fire of Gehenna.[10] In the Christian Articles of Faith, 1 Cor. 3:11–16 was considered to be the basis of a belief in purgatory fire. The Apostle Paul refers there to Jesus Christ as the foundation upon which each man builds his work:

> Now if anyone builds on the foundation with gold, silver, precious stones, wood, hay, stubble—each man's work will become manifest; for the Day will disclose it, because it will be revealed with fire, and the fire will test what sort of work each one has done. . . . Do you not know that you are God's temple and that God's spirit dwells in you?

The fire "tests" here the work of man, that which is eternal in it and that which is ephemeral. The fire which either "punishes" (hell) or purges or "tests" (purgatory) was, for a long time, not more precisely differentiated.[11] This was also the case with the in-between state which was at first not always described as a place of fire but rather as a *refrigerium* (a place of refreshment), where water flows.[12] Clement of Alexandria (died before 215) and Origen (died 253 or 254) were early advocates of the purgatory idea.[13] Hell, for Origen, is only a temporal place of limited punishment; he rejects the idea of eternal damnation. But purgatory serves as a *katharsis*, a psychic purification, and there souls are informed of the existence of something better. Only for those who cannot be taught is purgatory a punishment.[14] St. Augustine expresses for the first time the belief that the dead can be assisted in the in-between state through the intercessory prayers of the living.[15] Clement of Alexandria introduced a further idea worth mentioning, that the fire burns forth from God or Christ, and that the passage through purgatory is a kind of fire baptism.[16] Whereas for some this fire is a punishment, for others it is a means of sanctification; in the latter case it does not burn but, as a spiritual fire, flows through the soul.[17] It is not concrete fire as we know it, but rather a *subtle spiritual* fire. This idea of Clement comes very close to a modern psychological understanding of the fire symbolism of the Beyond.

*Fig. 9:* The "fire lake" with stele-like "wrappings" (mummies), from which emerge heads with the beards of gods.

The Christian ideas harken back quite clearly to the old Egyptian symbolism and they appear there in their original, primitive vividness. In the Egyptian world of the dead, there is a fire lake or fire hole (also called a fire island), the water of which is at the same time fire. Osiris "breathes through the unapproachable water of this fire hole." [18] The sun god Re speaks to the dead about this lake: "Its water belongs to you, but its fire is not directed against you, its heat is not directed against your dead body." [19] Evil ones, on the other hand, are tortured and burned by this fire, [20] and in this respect the fire-water "tests" everything which is in it.

From a psychological point of view, the fire is not to be understood concretely, of course. It was used by the old alchemists as a symbol, for they equated it with its opposite, the water, thereby obviously understanding it as a mystical fire. In itself fire is a symbol for psychic energy. It symbolizes that unknown psychic something which manifests itself in drives, wishes, volitions, affects, attention, capacity for work, etc., and their expressed degrees of intensity. [21]

Seen historically, our understanding of physical and psychic energy has emerged from the concepts of mana, mulungu, orenda, wakanda, manitu, etc., which primitive man understood to characterize everything that was uncanny, powerful, creative, extraordinarily effective, sacred—such as the lightning, a special tree or animal, the personality which radiated from a chieftain, etc. We recognize in this primitive concept what today we call psychic and physical energy, which for the primitive were not yet separated. Only after a long process of historical development did the modern understanding of physical energy develop out of the original concept of energy.[22] Heraclitus' mind-given fire corresponds to such a still relatively original idea of energy: "This ordered universe (*cosmos*) which is the same for all, was not created by any one of the gods or by mankind, but it was ever and is and shall be ever-living Fire, kindled in measure and quenched in measure."[23] In the Stoic philosophy this concept developed into the idea of a fiery spirit (*pneuma*) which fills the universe and is the divinity itself. In antique and medieval alchemy this ancient idea continued to exist in the image of Mercury, who was seen as a mysterious elementary fire, a life spirit present in all things, or as a creator nature spirit.[24] This fire spirit became the foundation of the so-called phlogiston theory in early chemistry, which then developed, as S. Samburski has shown, into the modern idea of the power field.[25]

In contrast with the quantitatively measurable energy of contemporary physics, psychic energy is something more qualitative, as Jung emphasizes,[26] an *intensity* which above all can only be perceived with feeling. Although, as he stresses,

> The psychic intensities and their graduated differences point to quantitative processes which are inaccessible to direct observation and measurement, they also have a sort of *latent physical* energy, since psychic phenomena exhibit a certain quantitative aspect. Could these quantities be measured, the psyche would be bound to appear as having motion in space, something to which the energy formula would be applicable. Therefore, since mass and energy are of the same nature, mass and velocity would be adequate concepts for characterizing the psyche so far as it has any observable effects in space; in other words, it must have an aspect under which it would appear as *mass in motion*. If one is unwilling to postulate a pre-established harmony of physical and psychic events, then they can only be in a state of *interaction*. But the latter hypothesis requires a psyche that touches matter at some point, and, conversely, a matter with a *latent psyche*.[27]

Jung's speculations indicate that in order to reach an understanding of the relationship between what, on the one hand, we call physical energy today, and psychic energy, on the other, parapsychology would have to be taken into consideration.

In my view, the alchemical fire symbolism alludes to an

energy intensity which characterizes the non-body-dominated psyche. One could imagine that in the process of dying this non-incarnated part of the psyche acquires the energy of the incarnated part and in this way is charged with an extremely high intensity. This is why the life elixir in the Komarios text is called "murderous," since at the end of life it helps to kill the body, as it were, or to render it inanimate and at the same time to animate the actual psyche (its eternal aspect), that is, to intensify it energically. The strong states of emotional excitement into which some dying people fall would, from this point of view, reflect a struggle between the psychic energy (fire = affects, emotions) which is still held in the fetters of the body, and the energy (intensification) of pure psychic life which is escaping from the body. In the case of violent death (murder, suicide) this struggle even seems to produce actual "explosive effects," as I once experienced myself. When I was about twenty-four years old, I lived in a rented room in the house of a sixteen-year-old girl and her nurse. One night I dreamed that a terrible explosion occurred. The nurse and I crouched behind a wall in order not to be hit by stones and lumps of earth flying about. When I awakened I was informed that during the night the girl had committed suicide with sleeping pills. In cases of suicide the life energy has not been used up naturally. As a result, death is like a sudden explosion which dangerously disturbs the environment; for, as we know, an explosion is nothing but a sudden liberation of highly charged energy.

Whereas, on the one hand the Beyond is often described mythologically as fiery—in either the positive or the negative sense—there are, on the other hand, equally many, if not more, witnesses who describe the resurrection of the dead as a rebirth from water, while in alchemy and in the Egyptian world of the dead, fire and water are sometimes explicitly equated.

In ancient China, as mentioned above, it was believed that the dead continued to live on in the ground water under the earth, and a similar idea predominated in Western antiquity. As Martin Ninck points out in his beautiful work, *Die Bedeutung des Wassers im Kult und Leben der Alten* (The Significance of Water in the Worship and Life of the Ancients), the ancient Greeks believed that all water springs from the depths of the earth where the large underground rivers Acheron and Kokytos and the Stygian Lake were located.[28] The lord of these waters was Hades, the underworld god. All things had their source in this sacred underground world; marriage, healing and new life belong to its realm. The black Styx, however, is in the land of the dead.[29] To drink its water brought death, but it also granted immortality if one drank it on certain days. The Elysian Fields and the Islands of the Blessed lie on the other side of the river of death.[30]

Water is associated with the "nocturnal states of the soul," as Ninck calls them—with dream, ecstasy, trance. Expressed in psychological language, it is an image of the collective unconscious. According to Timarchus,[31] dead souls wander about on this dream-sea like swimming, luminous points or stars; they stream through the depths and upward toward the moon, which is the residing place of purified souls.[32] As Oceanus, this water encircles the cosmos and is the origin of all life, even of the entire world. Zosimos[33] called water the "round element," $\Omega$ (omega).[34] This may presumably be traced back to the Egyptian idea that Osiris represents a round water element. A text for the protection of Osiris reads as follows: "You are large and green, like your name, 'Large Green Ocean.' Truly you are as great and round as the circle which embraces the Hanebu (islands). Truly you are as round and mighty as the 'round, mighty sea.' "[35] One is reminded here of the dream described earlier in which the dying man hesitated to enter a large blue eggshaped air liquid.

The Komarios text also speaks of waters flooding over the dead body in the underworld, before it is reborn in its glorified form. In the Egyptian Book of the Dead it is said that the deceased comes to the "hill of the water":

> Oh, hill of water, those who have died have no power over you, for your water is fire, your waves are fire. . . . If I could only possess you and drink from your stream! . . . I greet you, O god, who is in the hill of water! I have come to you, so that you may give me possession of the water, so that I may drink from the stream, as you have done for that great god for whom the flood comes, for whom plants are renewed, living creatures grow and vegetation flourishes. . . . Grant that the flood comes to me.[36]

This inundation was, by analogy, equated by the Egyptians
with the natron bath into which they placed the dead body at
the beginning of the mummification process. Thus a coffin text
runs as follows: "O, Osiris NN, come down and purify yourself,
together with Re, in the Natron Sea, and wrap yourself in the
garments of life." [37] The word "natron" is derived from the
Egyptian *n-t-r-*, which means "god," "divine." [38] So the immer-
sion of the dead body in a natron solution literally meant a deification, the transformation of the deceased into the god Osiris.

Furthermore, in the embalmment liturgy, the hieroglyph for
the god of the Nile was drawn on the bandages of the left hand
of the deceased, while the officiant repeated the following for-
mula:

> O, Osiris NN, the Nile, the great god, comes to you, in order
> to fill your offering with cool water. He gives you . . . Nun
> (the primal water) which comes from the cavern, the swirling
> water which comes from both mountains. You drink from
> them and they satisfy you. Your body is filled with fresh
> water, your coffin is filled with the tide, your throat is over-
> flowing. . . . You are Nun, the oldest one, the father of the
> gods. [39]

In the sixth of the "Vigil Hours of Osiris," the officiant carried
a vessel of Nile water. It was understood to be the same water as
that of Nun, the primal ocean, out of which all creation
emerged. The officiant called out: "Here is your substance, O
gods of Nun, that which makes it possible for you to live in his
name, the living one. . . . This water begets you as it begets Re,
every day; it makes it possible for you to be Chepera (scarab)." [40]

In the Isis procession described at the end of the *Metamor-
phoses*, Apuleius tells us that the most holy object carried in the
procession was a vessel full of Nile water. This is the previously
mentioned Osiris Hydreios, a new symbol which appeared in
Graeco-Roman Egypt (first century A.D.). It represented a kind
of matrix out of which the dead would be reborn and presumably, at the same time, an image of the goddess Isis, who begets
the dead once again. The vessel contains water from the Nile,
from that primal water, Nun, out of which, according to the
Egyptian view, all the gods emerged at the creation of the uni-

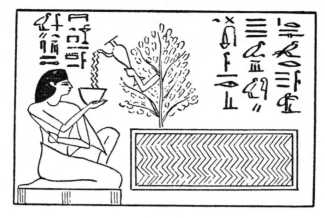

*Fig. 10:* The passage through water. Here the deceased drinks water in order "not to be burned out in the fire." Drinking water also plays a role in the embalmment liturgy: ". . . your body is filled with fresh water."

verse. As Nun, the primal waters from which all creation emerged, this water, which is also fire, is, in addition, a symbol of the collective unconscious. It would then figure as a matrix of images and symbolic insights, whereas fire would be more representative of its emotional quality.[41]

Both of these aspects of the unconscious appear in death experiences reported by Moody and Hampe. In describing their experiences, the patients were often overcome by profound emotions of bliss or of suffering. They emphasized time after time that they were unable to find words to describe their feelings adequately. They experienced an inexpressible emotion (fire).

On the other hand, these experiences often depict a kind of *flowing* of light, colors, images, souls, which are not clearly discernible in detail. They have a greater resemblance to the water aspect of the unconscious:

> A woman goes first through a tunnel: "I had to search for my escort somewhere in there, where the dark blue grew toward me from the opening of this tunnel. The hum became brighter and more beautiful. The colors, too, became clearer and seemed to merge into a game of a thousand colorful shades,

and then to fall apart again like the colors in a bouquet. Every color had a sound. And all those colors and sounds together produced a wonderful music which filled me and drew me forward."[42]

Or:

More and more I became enveloped in a magnificent blue sky with pink clouds and soft violet sounds. I floated along in this ideal atmosphere, smoothly and painlessly.[43]

Or:

In an unconscious state I saw in front of me pictures of myself in which all of the colors of the rainbow ran into one another.[44]

This streaming element is apparently met with very frequently in near-death experiences. It corresponds to the water aspect of the unconscious. Hindu burials, in which the ashes of the dead are scattered in the Ganges, or the Balinese custom of taking the ashes out to sea in a boat and scattering them there, express symbolically the idea of a redeeming dissolution, of a return to the primal ocean. At the same time, the symbolism represents the water aspect of the unconscious, something in which "the images of creation" float, somehow more beautiful and intense than in a dream, but even less comprehensible.

Let us return here to the dream of the dying man who was "on or in a skyblue air liquid" which had the shape of an egg. He felt that he was "falling into the blue, into the universe" and was afraid that he would be dissolved in it. But small blue cloths floating nearby enfolded and held him (after which he observed the Christmas tree). In a similar manner an aged man sent Jung the following dream:

He meets two . . . guides who lead him to a building where he finds many people, among them his father, stepfather, and his mother, who gives him a kiss of welcome. He has to go on a long climb ending at the edge of a deep precipice. A voice commands him to leap; after several desperate refusals he obeys and finds himself swimming "deliciously into the blue of eternity."[45]

Jung interprets this dream as a preparation for death and points out to the dreamer the Hindu belief that the dying rise upward to the cosmic Atman. "There is no loneliness, but all-ness or infinitely increasing completeness."[46]

The blue "air liquid" is a strange image which also appears in the work of a student of Paracelsus, the alchemist Gerhard Dorn. For Dorn, the entire alchemical opus culminates in the production of the so-called *caelum*, "the inner sky." He under-stood this to refer to the extracted quintessence of the life of the body, the inner truth which, as "God's exact image," lies hidden in the innermost recesses of man. If one distills and then rotates this liquid, one sees how it floats upward, translucently bright and of the purest "colour of the air."[47] In this way the mysteri-ous inner sky becomes visible. The production of this blue tinc-ture represented for Dorn the highest stage of the *coniunctio* (union of opposites), a union with the divine world spirit. Jung interprets it in the following way: "The whole of the conscious man is surrendered to the self, to the new centre of personality which replaces the former ego."[48]

The alchemical texts report that this, however, would only be an introductory stage, to be followed by further important trans-formations. It is an initial liberation from the bonds of the body, from the wishes and desires of the ego, from the narrow world to which consciousness, restricted by our cerebral bonds, confines us during our lifetime. But this seems to reflect only one initial stage of the event of death. Someone who was revived after being technically dead describes it in the following way:

> The condition in which I found myself was characterized by a feeling of extraordinary peace, but also by something quite different, that is, *by a premonition of great events, of an even further transformation.* But apart from my sudden return to the oper-ating table, there is nothing further to report.[49]

Many other similar reports contain a suggestion of the exis-tence of a further "threshold," from which apparently there would be no return.[50]

The Egyptian liturgy of the dead and the traditional symbols of alchemy describe further stages, of course, such as a return of the soul to the body, not to its old body but to a "form" of the same which, in the meantime, had been sublimated and transformed. We must therefore ask ourselves, what exactly happens to the old body while the soul has temporarily escaped from it into an ecstatic state?

# 7.
# The Sacrifice or Treatment of the Old Body

*A*ccording to the Komarios text, before spirit and soul can return to the body the latter must go through a transformation. First of all, there seems to be an indication that something like a dissolution or sacrifice of the old body must occur; it is to be tortured or fire tested, or the like. The man whose anima dream was cited on p. 51 reported the following final dream to his analyst just before dying:

> A man, either the dreamer or his best friend, was condemned to be executed and the dreamer offered to be the executioner. He did this hoping that he might save the man's life, for he considered him to be innocent. He had a sharp knife in his hand and had to make it look as though he wanted to kill the man, for if it became apparent that he wanted to save him, then he would have to pay with his own life. He cut down along the spine, then turned the man over. As he did so, he heard the bones crack and was afraid he might have cut too deeply. At that moment he awoke, with a strong feeling (even though this was not mentioned at all in the dream) that he would never be able to satisfy the girl he loved.[1]

In interpreting this dream, on the basis of the dreamer's associations,[2] Barbara Hannah points out that the friend who is to be sacrificed symbolizes a side of the dreamer that has remained far too youthful, a side which would still like to "catch up" on concrete sexual adventures with women. The knife which he uses in the dream had been used in reality to give the deathblow to animals when he was hunting. Apparently he should give the deathblow to this far too juvenile inner trait and stop trying to protect it secretly. Furthermore, as Hannah adds, "the one to be sacrificed also symbolizes the dreamer's egotistic willfulness, his wish to follow his own desires, rather than yield to the 'will of God,' to the laws of the inner self."[3] The too-youthful, sexually lustful side of the young man can also be seen as an identification with the body and its impulses. In a certain sense, then, the killing of that part of himself would also be a sacrifice to the body. To sacrifice, however, means to give up something in favor of a higher authority, usually that of a god or gods. *Basically, it is a sacrifice of egocentricity.*[4]

A man who was seriously wounded in World War II and who lay in a coma for a long period of time finally recovered and reported that

> he heard his sister saying that he had only two hours to live. "At that moment I suddenly felt a sensation of fear. I became aware of an intense, agonizing inner struggle, *the final struggle of the soul before the sacrifice.* The struggle took place in full consciousness. I will always keep the memory of that moment. I pray to God that it may never fade from my memory. . . . If one must leave this life courageously, then one must live it courageously."[5]

A "sacrifice" of the body in the sense of its deification is also to be found in the Egyptian mummification ritual. In the Cairo Museum and in the Louvre, there are two versions of old, unfortunately damaged, and in places not quite legible, instructions on how the dead should be dissected and embalmed.[6] Every part of the body is to be anointed at the same time with special oils and plant extracts. These oils and plant extracts are, however, "secretions" of the gods. A partial description of these instructions is as follows:

> Then anoint his head twice with good oil of myrrh and address him: "O, Osiris, the oil of myrrh which comes from Punt is put upon you in order to enhance your aroma through the god's aroma. The secretion which is upon you comes from Re, and it comes (in this way) to beautify (you). . . . Your soul walks on the land of the gods, upon your body. Horus is on you, he who comes from the myrrh oil, out of Osiris." The anointment of the body which produces a union with the god Osiris follows at this point. Then the entrails are placed in four Canopic jars, so that "the anointments of the mummy (of this god) can penetrate the limbs of the god." Then the spine is soaked with oil. After these anointments, he is addressed: "O, Osiris NN, take unto yourself this oil . . . take unto yourself (this) life's liquid. . . . Take unto yourself this (fat) of the gods, the secretion which came from Re, the emission which came from Schow (Schu, the air god), the sweat which came from

*Fig. 11:* "Treatment" of the body. Anubis, the jackal-headed Egyptian god of the dead, at the embalmment of the corpse of Osiris. To the right, Hathor giving instructions.

Geb (the earth god), the god's limbs which came from Osiris," etc. "To you, NN, come gold and silver, lapis lazuli, and malachite. To you come faience *(thn)* to transfigure your face *(thn)* and carnelian *(hnm)* to strengthen *(shn)* your movements. . . . To you, NN, come the garments which sprang from the eye of Horus, the beautiful secretions of Sobk (the crocodile god Suchos, the "master of the house of life"). . . . To you comes the robe from the temple of Sobk. It guides your path ·in Nun (the primal waters) and it adorns your limbs with its beauty, so that you are like Re when he steps up and steps down, and you do not cease to exist in eternity." Then one lays the mummy on its back and gilds its fingernails. The fingers are wrapped with linen bandages, each of which is attributed to a specific god. At this point the entire body is wrapped in bandages, then the head is anointed again. "Your head comes to you so that it will not be separated from you; it comes to you and does not separate itself (from you) in eternity." The hands are then shaped in such a way that they can "catch" or "get hold of" all the gods, the legs so that they can walk again. "The clothes of the gods are put upon your arms and the splendid robes of the goddesses on your limbs, so that your arms will be strong and your legs powerful." The text ends: "To you, Osiris NN, comes the incense, which came from Horus, the myrrh, which came from Re, the natron, which came from Nechbet, the anchjemi plants, which came from Osiris, the resin, which came from the great god, the gum, which came from the blessed Wennofre (Osiris). . . . You walk over an earth of silver and a ground of gold, you are buried on a slope of malachite. . . . You see your name in every region, your soul in the sky, your body in the Duat (underworld), your statues in the temples. You live in eternity and are forever young. O, Osiris NN, may your name endure and remain magnificent in the temple of Amon-Re, the king of gods, the holy image, the chief of all gods in eternity."[7]

This text informs us that in the Egyptian view the mummy is transformed into a "transfigured one." This is a chemical process of deification. The body of the deceased becomes, at the same time, a multitude of gods. However, in the image of the sun god it is also a unity of all gods. In psychological language, the dead body is transformed into an image of the collective unconscious *and*, in its aspect of oneness, into the Self. From the Egyptian point of view, the *ka* (shadow, double) and the *ba* (spiritual individuality) of the dead man are later united with this transfigured body, and together they become an inseparable unity. The resurrection is thus a unification of the individual self with the collective self; at the same time it is also an incorporation of both of them into the body in transfigured form.

We find a further example of the archetypal motif of a treatment of the body in the Edinger dream series. One of the dreams reported there is as follows:

As in Ginsberg's *Legends of the Jews*,[8] where God was in personal communication with various individuals, He seemed to have assigned me a test, distasteful in every way, for which I was in no way fitted, technically or emotionally. First I was to search for and find a man who was expecting me,[9] and together we were to follow exactly the instructions. The end result was to become an abstract symbol beyond our comprehension, with religious, or sacred, or tabu connotations. The task involved removing the man's hands at the wrists, trimming them and uniting them to make a hexagonal shape. Two rectangles, one from each hand were to be removed, leaving windows of a sort. The rectangles themselves were also symbols of great value. The results were to be mummified, dried-up and black. All of it took a long time, was extremely delicate and difficult. He bore it stoically as it was his destiny as well as mine, and the end result, we believed, was what was demanded. When we looked at the symbol that had resulted from our labors, it had an impenetrable aura of mystery about it. We were both exhausted by the ordeal.[10]

As Edinger points out, by referring to the alchemical motif of dismemberment, hands represent the instrument of the conscious will. To have them cut off would mean an experience of the impotence of the ego, or in Jung's words, "a defeat for the ego."[11] The hexagon which is then produced is an image of the Self, perhaps also of a primitive mask representing God's countenance. Six generally signifies a union of opposites. What is again important for us here is the sacrifice of physical man as carrier of the ego-will, through which he or his cut-off hands, that is, his activity, becomes the vessel or symbol of the Self. The analogy to the mummification process in Egypt is directly expressed in the dream.

Mark Pelgrin provides another example in this dream of a dying woman:

I saw vividly a number of very serious men, as though in a solemn ritual, waiting for me to come along on a stretcher on an open veranda that faced a courtyard. They were dressed in bright colors, some like silken jockey clothes. All were waiting for some work to do in the courtyard, some very important dignified work on me. There was a vague impression of an altar there to which I was taken *to be sacrificed to the gods, to be worked on by the powers within in some healing way.*[12]

This dream seems to me to point once again to a deification of the body similar to that codified in the Egyptian ritual—a transformation of the body, a healing which sublimates the body from within and at the same time unites its various parts with the different archetypes. Occasionally, the symbol of an animal represents the dead body, as we saw in the dream of the decomposing horse. A death dream that a correspondent sent to Jung, for instance, contains this motif:

> A magic horse . . . had been killed in battle . . . whose entrails (the dreamer) carries around for many years. Then he goes down some stairs and meets the resuscitated horse coming up. The horse devours all its own entrails, and is ready for the dreamer to mount.[13]

Jung answered:

> The dream of the horse represents the union with the animal soul, which you have missed for a long time. The union produces a peculiar state of mind, namely an unconscious thinking that enables you to realize the natural progress of the mind in its own sphere. You can understand it as the natural thought process in the unconscious or as an anticipation of postmortal mental life.[14]

In other words, this means that the life of archetypal images and ideas is actually hidden in the horse (the animal soul in the body); and that through the sacrifice and the carrying of the entrails (compare with Mithra's carrying of the bull), this hidden spiritual aspect of the body-soul, that is, of the collective unconscious, becomes possible to experience, a spiritual life which seems to exist beyond death.

The idea that individual parts of the body can be coordinated with certain gods (archetypes) is very richly developed in the Far East. In the Chinese taoistic view of the world, for instance, man is a microcosm (as in Western astrology) whose subdivisions correspond exactly with the "floors" of Heaven and with its constellations.[15] A subtle psychophysical life energy called *ch'i* circulates throughout this physical cosmos.[16] Every organ, indeed every smallest part of the body, has its deity, and this deity is described as the "highest officer" or the "highest function" of that part. If the deity should abandon its organ, the latter then ceases to function and decays. Such divinities of the body must, therefore, be taken care of through meditation, through one's diet, etc. One must "unify them through the body," in order to attain long life, even immortality.[17]

The organs are also the seat of the "heavenly feelings";[18] that is, feelings such as benevolence, displeasure, sorrow, and joy are determined by the heavens in much the same way that certain basic moods are seen by us as having been caused by planetary influences. In this spiritual hierarchy, the heart is the monarch in which spirit and clarity have their source; the lungs are the seat of the official who is in charge of organization and order; the liver is the seat of strategy and planning; the gall bladder of decision-making and judgment; the large intestine of instruction in the correct way of doing things and of transformation and change; the small intestine of development; the kidneys of the power of action, etc. These seats correspond to images of the stars in the macrocosm.

Certain symbolic animals are also present in each organ: a white tiger in the lungs, a turtle and a snake in the gall bladder, a dragon in the liver, a phoenix in the spleen, a red bird in the heart, and a white twoheaded deer in the liver. One can observe all of these creatures directly by looking within oneself. Because the macrocosmic deities often wander around and are consequently more difficult to observe, it is easier to establish contact through meditation with those divinities which are continually present within our bodies and who are secretly identical with the cosmic deities. In this way we can finally reach the universal meaning of tao.

Similar ideas are also to be found in Tibetan medicine and in Indian tantrism. The entire system of Indian tantric yoga is based on the idea that the body is an image of the cosmos, is a complete union of the spiritual and the material. The yogi realizes that he is himself the divine universe.[19] Inside the material body he possesses a subtle body, composed of the omnipresent psychophysical energy which concentrates in special "knot-points" (chakras). In the puja (an act of veneration in each ceremony), as well as in the tantric ritual, the individual making the offering "honors" himself by covering certain parts of his body with flower garlands, ointments, perfumes, etc. In this way he completely transforms his nature into something divine; every part of his body receives divine nature, exactly as in the Egyptian mummification process, the only difference being that this transformation is performed on a still-living person. In this way the subtle body is the invisible vehicle of this transformation.

Yogis moreover often remain for a long time at the places of ritual fires in order to achieve a "symbolic transformation" in which one gives up all egocentric impulses.[20] The individual parts of the body, in their cosmic form, then become divinities which together constitute the Cosmic Deity.[21]

Not only the practitioners of tantric yoga but every Indian who "renounces" the world (sannyasin) undergoes such a transformation. Each cosmic body form emerges and its life-breath rises with the sacrificial fire, after which the initiate is regarded as dead to the world.[22] He has, as it were, anticipated his physical death in the sacrificial ritual. The important thing for our consideration here is the fact that each individual part of the body possesses a kind of soul or divinity or symbolic animal of its own. What we call the collective unconscious today appears there to be projected onto the individual parts of the body. Admittedly this is perhaps more than just a projection. We know that dreams with snakes or insects, for instance, often go together with disturbances of the sympathetic nervous system. It is therefore quite possible that certain archetypes would indeed somehow be specifically connected with certain functions or areas of the body. This is, to a large extent, an unresearched area of depth psychology.[23] Seen historically, however, there has always and everywhere existed a belief in such connections.

Similar views are to be found in the West in astrologically influenced medicine, although it is less systematized there than in the East. According to the astrology of antiquity, specific celestial gods and signs of the zodiac "govern" different parts of the body; for instance, Scorpio rules over the genital organs, Capricorn over the knees, Pisces over the feet, etc. These views were held without any great change throughout the Middle Ages. They were repressed, it is true, with the victory of Christian monotheism, as they also were in Islam, but they were never completely eradicated and had a great rebirth during the Renaissance. These ideas were once again very vividly expressed by Paracelsus. In keeping with the tradition, man for him was a microcosm with an endosomatic heaven, as it were, which he called the "firmament," "astrum" or "sydus,"[24] This is a part or a content of the visible body and is the source of all natural illumination by the *lumen naturale*.[25] Saturn influences the spleen and its therapy, Jupiter the liver, the sun the heart and the imagination, Venus the kidneys, Mars the gall bladder and the power of individual development, the moon the brain, etc. Illnesses, too, all belong to such star constellations. Furthermore, the Archeus (Archasius), a creatively nourishing spirit, operates in the stomach.

The "astral body" as a whole forms the "Adech," that is, the cosmic "greater man" who lives in every individual.[26] Characteristically enough, Paracelsus also refers to the mummification process of the Egyptians, who, as he says, use an agent (balsam) to render the mortal body immune to decomposition and a substance (the flower *cheyri*) which insures long life for it.[27] With such means, it is said, the *imago Dei*, The "spiritual inner man" is reproduced and renewed and this part of man is imperishable and outlives death.

In alchemy, as Jung points out, it is a question of the liberation of the sphere of nature in man which was denied and suppressed by Christianity.

I have found two cases among the reports of dying people which seem to allude to such alchemical-astrological ideas. The first comes from the prominent doctor and parapsychologist, Sir Auckland Geddee:

On Saturday, the 9th of November, one minute before midnight, I began to feel very ill and at two o'clock I suffered an acute gastro-enteritis. By eight o'clock I had all the symptoms of an acute poisoning; I could hardly count my pulse or my breathing. I wanted to ring for help but I realized that I could no longer do so, so I gave up the attempt quite calmly. It was clear to me that I was very ill and I went over my financial situation very briefly. During all this time, consciousness seemed in no way to be clouded. But suddenly I noticed that consciousness had separated itself from another consciousness which was also in me. In order to describe this phenomenon better, let me call them A-consciousness and B-consciousness. In all that follows, my ego and my A-consciousness were attached to each other. I noticed that the B-personality belonged to my body. As my physical condition became more and more serious and my heart scarcely beat at all, I realized that the B-consciousness, which belonged to the body, began to show signs of a complicated structure, that is, it constructed itself out of physical sensations in the head, the heart and the entrails. These components then became independent of each other and the B-consciousness began to fall apart, whereas the A-consciousness, which was now I, myself, seemed to be completely outside the body, which I could now observe. Gradually I realized that I could not only see my body and the bed in which I lay, but also everything in the house and the garden, and then I noticed that I could not only see objects in the house but also things in London and in Scotland, wherever I directed my attention. From a source unknown to me, which I called my Mentor, I was instructed that I was completely free in a time dimension of space, in which the "now" was, in a way, equivalent to the "there" in the ordinary three-dimensional space of everyday life. I saw then that the doctor had been called and he gave my lifeless body an injection of camphor . . . and I was drawn back. . . . I went back reluctantly, back to my body.[28]

When a woman patient was brought back to life by her doctors from a diabetic coma, she reported:

I saw that I was being carried away in small parts. All of my parts had different colors. Everything was separated from the trunk of my body. Over there lay the liver . . . here the heart . . . and there the lungs. They formed a color game, profound and beautiful. And I saw that I was carried away to the kingdom of light. (When she had to return to her body, the organs were together again.)[29]

Whereas Geddee does not pursue the disintegration of B-consciousness any further, this woman *is* interested in her disintegrating organs. She especially emphasizes their colors, the beautiful "color game" which others also describe, not so much in connection with the body as with their experience of the Beyond.

If we try to view these modern experiences in the light of the statements of the Egyptian ritual for the dead, there arises for me the following hypothesis: During mummification the organs of the body were assigned specific gods, that is, psychologically different archetypes of the collective unconscious. The latter seem to be projected, as it were, onto the body or to be incarnated in it. Body-consciousness (Geddee's B-consciousness) seems to dissolve at the approach of death, like the dead in the mummification ritual who are first dissolved in the primal waters of Nun. During the ritual for the dead, however, a further step is taken. The deified (transfigured) body is reassembled into a new unity—newly united with the sun god Re and with the other soul parts. Geddee's A-consciousness would correspond in Egypt to the mentor, the voice of instruction, the *ba* soul, which, for example, appears in the famous Egyptian text, "The Dialogue of a World-Weary Man with His Ba," as an instructing spirit.

I believe therefore that Hampe is not necessarily right when he assumes that B-consciousness dissolves definitively. It seems that perhaps only a momentary dissolution takes place for the purpose of transformation. This, however, appears to be dependent somehow on human effort, on an *opus*.

Hampe reports another experience of death which poses a riddle for me. It is the account of a patient from the Oestersund Clinic for Infectious Diseases in Sweden:

I was in a completely different world. . . . I was standing on a highly elevated place. Although it was dark around me I felt comfortable and I managed to find my way here and there with ease. Then as I looked around me I could see that, in front of me, in the dark, there was quite a high wall. On this side of the wall I saw a staircase which went along the wall, close to it. As it moved upward toward the right and further away from me, it was more and more illuminated until it disappeared in a strong, clear light. From where I was standing, I saw, not too far away from me, a little brown man, wrinkled and frail. He wanted to go up the staircase into the light. But it looked as though he was not moving at all. I noticed, on closer observation, that he was carrying a burden on his back. It looked like a sack and was obviously so heavy that his knees shook under the weight. I said to myself immediately that I ought to help the poor fellow, for I felt that I had some connection with him and was responsible for him. At the same time, however, I realized that from where I was standing I could do very little for him.

The little man had not yet advanced very far on his dark way up toward the light. All around him it was black; the pathway seemed to be made of soft coal dust. It became bright only a bit further up. I felt sympathy for the little man.

Although I was alone with this miserable creature I felt another presence nearby. There was a voice in me which immediately and clearly answered everything I asked in my thoughts. "How do we get out of here?" From quite nearby the voice gave me the following answer: "You have always wanted to experience great things and do many things, haven't you? Well, now you have the chance!" "But I cannot manage it," I answered. The voice said, "You can leave your body, which is lying down there. The pathway upwards is open for you!" "But isn't it unfair to leave the poor wretch halfway on his way to the light?" "You must help him with your will!" "It's a tempting offer, to leave the body," I said, but all the same I made up my mind to fight.

I fought for a long time with myself. Then I looked again at the little man. He had advanced a bit further in the meantime, but as I watched him he did not seem to move again. I discovered then that he had grown a little and the sack seemed to have become smaller and lighter. The manikin had proper legs now, the knees were no longer bent. I was glad that I had not deserted the creature, and turned again to my "friend." "I believe we are going to make it; you have strengthened me by remaining close to me." The voice answered, "You see, a will to fight honestly and fairly always leads to the goal."

The answer was vague, but right away I felt warmth and gratitude rise up within me. I had encountered my "friend." He had awakened hope in me. I will never forget him. From that moment on I never felt separated from him; he stood by my side; he spoke out of me, out of myself. I saw that the little man below me no longer carried a burden. And then I found myself in my own body once again, here in the clinic. The whole episode seemed ridiculous and contemptible to me.[30]

Hampe interprets this primarily as an effort of the experiencing subject to cooperate in the recovery of his body during a blood transfusion. Therefore he sees the little brown man as the sick body, the burden he interprets as a piece of the patient's past which has to be coped with. I believe this to be correct for the most part, but the vision points to something even more precise. The "burden" and the "coal dust," rather than the "little man," are to be understood as the real body, which indeed is, to a great extent, made of carbon. The little man, on the contrary, seems to me to represent not the body itself but a kind of "life spirit" which animates the body. The experience, or rather the little man, amplified mythologically, refers to the alchemical tradition, especially to the visions of Zosimos, for there, in the center of the vision, is also a homunculus *(anthroparion)*.[31] Zosimos sees in a dream a sacrificial priest standing on an altar that is shaped like a bowl with fifteen steps leading up to it. The priest says of himself that he is Ion, "the priest of the inner sanctuaries" and he submits himself "to an unendurable torment." Then he speaks of a man who came at early morning, scalped and dismembered him, after which he "was burned upon the fire of the art, till I perceived by the transformation of the body that I had become spirit."[32] Then the priest spewed forth all his own flesh and Zosimos "saw how he changed into the opposite of himself, into a mutilated anthroparion, and he tore his flesh with his own teeth, and sank into himself."[33] Zosimos then asks himself how this could be connected with the goal of alchemy, with "the composition of the waters." He falls asleep again and sees once more the bowl-shaped altar in which a numberless multitude of people are now being boiled. A homunculus, who is also a barber, explains to him that this is "the transformation . . . the place of the operation *[askeseos]* called embalming *[taricheia]*. Those who seek to obtain the art enter here, and become spirits *[pneumata]* by escaping from the body."[34] Later the homunculus is also referred to as the lead, and as the priest who sacrifices and is sacrificed and is transformed gradually, in the course of subsequent visions, from a brazen man to a silver man and finally to a golden man sitting on a round temple built from *one* white stone. Within the temple there is "a spring of the purest water, sparkling like the sun."[35]

The homunculus appears here as the guiding spirit *(spiritus rector)* of a transformation process within man, a process which is also called mummification *(taricheia)*. This transformation is a spiritualization and also—as we know from the Egyptian sources—a deification of the body. The Zosimos text suggests repeatedly, however, that the guardian spirit of the embalming represents at the same time that which is itself being transformed; it is bodily matter *and* at the same time that which sublimates it into spirit, *a kind of quintessence of the material body*. The production or liberation of such a quintessence of the life of the body remained the principle effort of alchemists over the centuries. Thus Paracelsus declared much later: "This is the spirit of truth, whom the world cannot comprehend without the inspiration of the Holy Ghost, or without the instruction of those who know him" "He is the soul of the world," moving all and preserving all. In his initial earthly form (that is, in his original Saturnine darkness), he is unclean, but he purifies himself progressively during the ascent through his watery, aerial, and fiery forms. Finally, in the fifth essence, he appears as the "clarified body." "This spirit is the secret that has been hidden since the beginning of things."[36]

In the Zosimos text, this spirit, Ion, is referred to as the priest of the innermost sanctuaries. Jung relates the name Ion to the Sabaen Jûnañ (son of Mercury) who was considered to be the founder of the alchemical art.[37] The name might also possibly point to Joun-Mutef, the name of the priest of the Sed celebration, who transformed the king into Osiris, that is, brought about his symbolic death and renewal. The word *joun* means "skin," "coat"(!), *mutef*, "his mother," which, according to A. Moret, alludes to rebirth symbolism.[38] In Seti's grave, the son of the king (representing the god Horus) is depicted as Joun-Mutef-priest. The Sed celebration serves for the renewal of the king, a symbolism which refers as well to the production of the lapis throughout the entire alchemical tradition.

In light of such historical amplification, the "little man" or the "poor wretch" in the vision of the Swedish patient reported by Hampe would be the *spiritus rector* of a process of spiritualization or of a *"sublimation" of the body's substance*, serving thereby to produce the *lapis philosophorum*, that is, it brings about much more than just physical healing. The voice in the vision actually says that the patient will be able to "experience great things and do many things," namely to observe the "great work" of alchemical transformation. Since this work is not Christian, it is understandable that the experiencing individual may hesitate to devote himself to it.

The voice of the "friend" in the vision leaves it up to the patient to choose whether he will go away into the light and into death, or whether he will participate in the efforts of the little man, but the voice praises him when he decides for the latter. This reminds one of the equally mysterious behavior of the *ba* (the immortal part of the soul) of that Egyptian World-Weary Man when, in their dialogue, the question arises as to whether the man should go on living or commit suicide. The *ba*, after using several parables to criticize the affective, impatient and despairing attitude of the World-Weary Man, does not end by giving him advice—that he should *not* kill himself—but says only:

> Now let the lamentation be; you, who belong to me, my brother! You may (continue to) weigh upon the brazier,[39] or you may again cling to life (according) as you will say. Wish me to stay here, if you have renounced the West, or else wish to attain the West and for your body to be given to the earth, and for me to settle here, after you have departed (this life): in any case we shall share home together.[40]

As Helmut Jacobson explains, this "home" for which the World-Weary Man searches is a state of "being one with" and "joined in human wholeness" with the *ba*, "the joining together of the human totality."[41] The patient cited by Hampe who had the vision of the "little man" also declares in a similar manner: "I had encountered my 'friend.' He has awakened hope in me. I will never forget him. From that moment on I never felt separated from him; he stood by my side; he spoke out of me, out of myself."[42]

Seen psychologically, this would mean that for the Self—the totality superordinate to the ego—for the inner divine man, the question of life and death becomes strangely indifferent. What is important is only the great work, the completion of inner wholeness, which is accomplished by connecting oneself with the Self. The decomposition of B-consciousness into the various inner organ components observed by Sir Auckland Geddee, when seen in this light, would be only the first dismemberment or the *separatio elementorum* of the alchemical work, a dismemberment which is apparently of the body but in truth is of the "inner man" who is projected onto the body, and which is followed by the recomposition of an immortal body.

The Egyptians carried out this symbolic process concretely on the dead body in the form of the embalming ritual, which indeed the Zosimos text also refers to explicitly in connection with the homunculus. So in this opus or process a part of the psychic energy is withdrawn from the coarse material body and reformed into a new breathlike (pneumatic) body. This, at any rate, was the basic intention of the alchemical tradition. In the death experiences reported by Hampe and Moody, aside from the vision of the little man, one finds no allusions to this stage of the process, probably because after it takes place there is generally no return to the old body. As we will see later, the weightless stone or the stone untouched by fire in the dream described earlier may perhaps be a hidden allusion to this event.

# 8.

# The Shifting Ego-Identity, Multiple Souls and Their Fixation in the Fruit

*W*hen one compares the near-death and dying experiences published by Moody, Osis, Hampe, and Sabom, one notices that the factors of ego and ego consciousness are often strangely shifting. In many accounts the survivor relates his entire experience from the ego point of view, that of an ego which seems to be equivalent to the normal ego of everyday life. This everyday ego is then confronted with a "voice" or with an "inner friend," who in Jungian psychology would be interpreted as a personification of the Self.

In some instances the everyday ego seems also to merge partially somehow with this Self being. Moody cites the case of a man who first met the "being of light" in a deep coma (caused by bronchial asthma): "It was just a ball of light, almost like a globe, and it was not very large, I would say no more than twelve to fifteen inches in diameter."[1] A hand, reaching out to him, invited him to come along so that he himself floated aloft and then moved with the light being here and there in the hospital room. "Now, immediately, when I had joined him . . . and had become a spirit myself, in a way we had been fused into one. We were two separate ones, too, of course. Yet, he had full control of everything that was going on as far as I was concerned."[2] An intimate association between ego and Self is described here *but not a complete merging of the two.*

In another report the everyday ego is so greatly altered that it closely resembles the Self:

My new ego was no longer the old familiar ego, but rather a sublimate of it, as it were, even if it did seem to me somehow familiar, like something I had always known but which had been deeply buried under a superstructure of fears, hopes, wishes and desires. This ego had nothing to do with the ego of this world. It was a spirit, absolute, unchangeable, indivisible, indestructible. Although absolutely unique, as individual as a fingerprint, it was at the same time part of an infinite, well-ordered whole.[3]

The two aspects, ego and Self, are almost completely united here, but the ego feeling remains *part* of a larger whole; it is not the whole itself. In his visions on the brink of death, Jung describes a similar change in his everyday ego:

> I had the feeling that everything was being sloughed away; everything I aimed at or wished for or thought, the whole phantasmagoria of earthly existence, fell away or was stripped from me—an extremely painful process. Nevertheless something remained; it was as if I now carried along with me everything I had ever experienced or done, everything that had happened around me. I might also say: it was with me, and I was it. I consisted of all that, so to speak. I consisted of my own history, and I felt with great certainty: this is what I am. "I am this bundle of what has been, and what has been accomplished."
>
> This experience gave me a feeling of extreme poverty, but at the same time of great fullness. There was no longer anything I wanted or desired. I existed in an objective form; I was what I had been and lived. At first the sense of annihilation predominated, of having been stripped or pillaged; but suddenly that became of no consequence. Everything seemed to be past, what remained was a *fait accompli*, without reference back to what had been. There was no longer any regret that something had dropped away or been taken away. On the contrary: I had everything that I was, and that was everything.[4]

Jung's altered, "objective" ego, which had "everything that (it) was," reminds one of Simon Magus' idea of that "fruit" of the life-tree which survives the destruction of the tree. This new ego seems to be a kind of lived quintessence, which at the same time is also a termination of life. Buddhism also teaches that our experiences and actions are transformed into "grain" which represents the "fruit of our deeds." This grain survives in an after-death dimension.[5] In the previously cited passage from Simon Magus, the fruit of the world-tree which survives death is God's image in the human soul—the Self, in Jungian language. The immortal *doppelgänger* in man is also referred to in the Persian religion as a fruit of man's lived faith. And finally the motif of the fruit also appears in modern dreams. The psychotherapist Liliane Frey relates a dream which illustrates this motif. It is the case of a dying eighty-year-old man who entertained doubts in consciousness about survival after death. Then shortly before he died he dreamed:

> A sick old plum tree unexpectedly bears a lot of fruit on one of its branches. At the edge of one bough there are even two golden plums. Full of joy, I show this miracle to my daughter and to my son.[6]

In alchemy the lapis is often described as the fruit of the sun tree and the moon tree, a final transfiguration of the life that has been lived and which is represented by the tree itself. This fruit or end result even seems capable of continuing to have effects in the collective unconscious. Thus a man who had suffered a great deal in his professional life dreamed a short time before his death:

> A voice speaking in an oriental language says to me: "Your work and your life, which you have endured consciously, have redeemed hundreds in your generation and will have an illuminating influence upon hundreds of generations to come."[7]

This dream seems to answer a question which is often of concern to any reflective person: Why must highly valuable "important" people often go unnoticed and unappreciated by the public at large and suffer thereby throughout their lives, whereas heartless, empty-headed individuals are praised by almost everyone? According to this dream, there exists an invisible compensation. Suffering and pain which are *consciously* lived often seem to have their own rewards—their fruit—but often only in the Beyond, as is indeed emphasized in Christian teaching. The difference, however, is that in the dream the image is not that of reward or punishment but of something more objective. Consciously lived suffering has a redeeming effect on the past and on the future of mankind, an effect which is exerted invisibly from the Beyond (from the collective unconscious). To understand this, however, is surely the highest reward which an individual may expect from life. In this connection, Edinger reports an impressive dream of a person fated soon to die:

> I have been set a task nearly too difficult for me. A log of hard and heavy wood lies covered in the forest. I must uncover it, saw or hew from it a circular piece, and then carve through the piece a design. The result is to be preserved at all cost, as representing something no longer recurring and in danger of being lost. At the same time, a tape recording is to be made describing in detail what it is, what it represents, its whole meaning. At the end, the thing itself and the tape are to be given to the public library. Someone says that only the library will know how to prevent the tape from deteriorating within five years.[8]

As Edinger interprets it, this object is a unique quintessence—the goal and completion of physical existence. This quintessence is to be deposited as a permanent increment to a collective or transpersonal library as a kind of "spirit treasury." In an astonishing way this resembles Simon Magus' idea of a "heavenly barn" into which the "fruit" is brought.

This fruit in the Beyond is often described as the philosopher's stone, as gold fruit, diamond body, etc., that is, as something static, completed, whereas ego consciousness, which is still living in time, experiences itself more as a "flow" of representations. In Jung's report, what seems to drop away from the everyday ego is the hoping, wishing, desiring, fearing, etc., that is, the affective emotional relation to the future; what remains is only that which was and is. This wishing, fearing, desiring, etc., seems to have its source in Geddee's B-consciousness, which appears to be closely related to the somatic realm.

Another of Moody's cases describes the relation of the "purified ego" to the Self (the being of light) in the following way: "When my heart stopped beating . . . I felt like I was a round ball and almost maybe like I might have been a little sphere—like a B-B—on the inside of this round ball. I just can't describe it to you."[9] This is an especially striking image, for it seems to describe the "correct" relation of the ego to the Self, that is, the ego is a part of the whole and is at the same time one with the whole. It is just this relation between ego and Self which Jungian depth psychology attempts to establish in every analysand during his or her lifetime.[10] For if the ego identifies with the Self, then it suffers an inflation. If it goes too far away from the Self, then it sinks into "wishing, hoping, fearing and desiring" and loses itself in the world. The above examples illustrate the strange and paradoxical relation between the purified ego and the Self. Sometimes the ego is described as identical with the Self, at other times as separate or as a smaller ball united with a larger one. As long as the everyday ego is not purified, it experiences itself as distinctly separate from the Self, whereas when it is completed it becomes to a large extent identical with the Self; however, the ego awareness which is necessary for the perception of the Self seems thereby not to cease. The ego, says Jung,

> is an essential part of the self, and can be used *pars pro toto* when the significance of consciousness is borne in mind. But when we want to lay emphasis on the psychic totality it is better to use the term "self." There is no question of a contradictory definition, but merely of a difference of standpoint.[11]

The image of the relation between ego and Self as a smaller ball within a larger one is beautifully represented in the above pre-death vision.

Something gets lost at death, however. Together with the cessation of affects, desires, and emotions, much of what one calls "human warmth" also seems to disappear. Sometimes one can observe this with dying people whose reactions are strangely "far away" and "detached," as if no human relation mattered any more.[12] What seems to cease therefore through the purification is the wishing, fearing, and desiring of the ego. This was made clear to me by an experience of my own, a dream which I had about three weeks after the death of my father. He died suddenly when I was absent from home, and I was naturally preoccupied with the problem of his departure. I had the following dream:

> It was about ten o'clock in the evening, dark outside. I heard the doorbell ring and "knew" at once somehow that this was my father coming. I opened the door and there he stood with

a suitcase. I remembered from the Tibetan *Book of the Dead* that people who died suddenly should be told that they are dead, but before I could say so he smiled at me and said: "Of course I know that I am dead, but may I not visit you?" I said: "Of course, come in," and then asked, "How are you now? What are you doing? Are you happy?" He answered: "Let me remember what you, the living, call happy. Yes, in your language, I am happy. I am in Vienna (his hometown which he loved and longed for all his life) and I am studying at the music academy." Then he went into the house, we climbed the stairs and I wanted to lead him to his former bedroom. But he said: "Oh, no, now I am only a guest," and went up to the guest-room. There he put his suitcase down and said: "It is not good for either the dead or the living to be together too long. Leave me now. Good night." And with a gesture he signalled me not to embrace him, but to go. I went into my own room, thinking that I had forgotten to put out the electric stove and that there was a danger of fire. At that moment I woke up, feeling terribly hot and sweating.

Jung interpreted this dream on the objective level, that is, as a dream concerning my real father.[13] He said that my father was in Vienna, his much beloved hometown; he had "gone home," as we often say symbolically of the dead. My father was musical but he had never perfected this gift; apparently he was then catching up with something he had neglected in life. But that strange remark about being "happy" is especially important. His present ideas about happiness are obviously quite different from those he had when he was alive. This reminds one of the Breton fairytale in which the living spectator thinks that Death slaps his wife brutally on the face, while she experiences the blows as loving kisses. Apparently feelings are so different after death that we can scarcely express them any longer in the language of the living.

Also noteworthy in this dream is the end motif of the over-heated stove and my feeling terribly hot upon awakening. Jung's interpretation was that being in touch with the "coldness" of the world of ghosts produced a strong physical counterreaction as a healing defense against the danger of contagion by the chill of death. He speaks further about this motif in a letter.[14] The recipient of the letter had felt the ghostly "presence" of his brother (who had died in an accident in West Africa) and had spoken with his ghost in a dream. In this dream the brother suddenly jumped into a lake and the dreamer observed a hill of ants. Then the contact was broken. The dreamer said it was like a telephone connection when the electric current is slowly fading away; one knows the other person is still there, but one hears his voice less and less distinctly. In his reply, Jung answered that he had really spoken with his dead brother.

> Naturally we can form no conception of a relatively timeless and spaceless existence, but, psychologically, and empirically, it results in manifestations of the continual presence of the dead and their influence on our dream life. I therefore follow up such experiences with the greatest attention, because they show many things we dream about in a very peculiar light, where "psychological" structures appear as existential conditions. This continual presence is also only relative, since after a few weeks or months the connection becomes indirect or breaks off altogether, although spontaneous re-encounters also appear to be possible later. But after this period the feeling of the presence of the dead is in fact broken off. The connection is not without its dangers because it entangles the consciousness of the living too much in that transcendental state, resulting in unconsciousness and dissociation phenomena. This is reflected in your dream-vision of the path leading down to the lake (the unconscious). There is an antheap, i.e., the sympathetic nervous system (= deepest unconsciousness and danger of dissolution of psychic elements in the form of milling ants) is becoming activated. . . .
>
> With regard to contact with your brother, I would add that this is likely to be possible only as long as the feeling of the presence of the dead continues. But it should not be experimented with because of the danger of a disintegration of consciousness. To be on the safe side, one must be content with spontaneous experiences. Experimenting with this contact regularly leads to the so-called communications becoming more and more stupid [15] or to a dangerous dissociation of consciousness. All the signs indicate that your conversation with your brother is a genuine experience which cannot be "psychologized." The only "psychological" disturbance in it is the lake and the antheap. That was evidently the moment when, perhaps from both sides, the exceedingly difficult contact between the two forms of existence could no longer be maintained.

There are experiences which show that the dead entangle themselves, so to speak, in the physiology (sympathetic nervous system) of the living. This would probably result in states of possession.[16]

My dream motif of the overheated stove would be (in contrast to this) a physiological defense against such a possible entanglement. *At any rate it is emphasized that the world of the living and the world of the dead should not come too close to each other, that they are somehow dangerous for each other.* The sphere of wishes, feelings and affects seems especially altered in the Beyond.

The ego of someone in a coma apparently loses not only its connection with the coarse material body, but also with the sphere of affects or emotions (fears, wishes, desires). Unlike some of the above cases, Jung perceived this primarily as a bereavement. Others have also emphasized the loneliness of this condition. One said: "It is an awesome, lonely feeling, a feeling of complete isolation. I knew that I was completely alone, by myself."[17] And another:

> I was aware the whole time of being alone, though, very alone —almost like I was a visitor from someplace else. It was like all relations were cut. I know—it was like there was no love or anything. Everything was just so—technical. I don't understand, really.[18]

Jung, too, refers to a strange cessation of human warmth in the Beyond, where, however, something like an objective relationship seems possible.

> In general, emotional ties are very important to human beings. But they still contain projections, and it is essential to withdraw these projections in order to attain to oneself and to objectivity. Emotional relationships are relationships of desire, tainted by coercion and constraint; something is expected from the other person, and that makes him and ourselves unfree. Objective cognition lies hidden behind the attraction of the emotional relationship; it seems to be the central secret. Only through objective cognition is the real *coniunctio* possible.[19]

The uncertainty which emerges in these witnesses as to what the ego and consciousness actually are and what their capacity for transformation is, has an extensive historical background. The majority of peoples who are close to nature believe that man has not just one but different souls which separate after death, sometimes completely.[20] What the ethnologists refer to as a soul is mostly an ego soul or a free soul. It is regarded as the focal point of thinking, it lives in the head or in the heart and survives death to live in a place in the Beyond.[21] (In our material this soul would correspond to the relation of the ego to the light being (Self) or the purified ego.) A further soul, the so-called "image soul," is a kind of mirror soul; it appears also in the shadow of man and is activated in dreams, in visions, and in unconsciousness. (According to the belief of some peoples it lives outside the individual during his lifetime as a bush soul or outer soul, or in an object or a container.) This soul also continues to exist after death as a ghost. In our context it would correspond to the Egyptian *ba*, which normally appears after death.

Numerous tribes living close to nature speak about another soul, a kind of "vital soul" or "breath soul." This is the force that activates the life of the organism; it is more physical than the image soul. According to the opinion of some tribes this soul also continues to exist but in another place, often a place like the underworld. According to other tribes, like the body it perishes.[22] Of course one must be very careful here in the use of the word "soul." It is not related in any way to our common understanding of the word. Images referring to it also vary, or they overlap. (For instance, in Egypt the "free soul" would refer more often to the *ba*, although sometimes, as shadow or mirror image, it would correspond rather to the *ka*.) The "vital soul" or "breath soul" would correspond in our context to Geddee's B-consciousness, or to the little man in the vision of the Swedish patient. Although many peoples believe in four, five or more (up to thirteen) souls in man,[23] a partition into two is more noticeably widespread. The two are usually a spiritual, free (not quite incarnated) soul and one more attached to the physical body. From the point of view of depth psychology, however, *both* kinds of soul are aspects of *one* psychic totality, the Self. It seems therefore as if the Self, the divine center in man, possesses two aspects, one nonincarnated, purely spiritual, timeless-eternal; the other demiurgical, manifesting itself in physical matter. To "redeem" the latter and reunite it with the eternal aspect *depends*, according to the alchemists, *on the efforts of man;* only with effort can one become completely whole. Seen in this light, the actual resurrection is just *this* union of the two aspects of the Self—a second death marriage. The thirteenth-century alchemist Petrus Bonus described this second union in the following way:

> In the conjunctional resurrection, the body becomes completely spiritual like the soul itself, and they become one, as when one mixes water with water, since there is no longer any difference between them, but rather a unity of all three, namely of spirit, soul and body, without separation, in eternity.[24]

A very close parallel idea of a duality that must be overcome is found in taoistic alchemy. Quite generally speaking, the Chinese assumed that when a man died a bipartition took place first,[25] in which his body soul *(p'o)* sinks downward, whereas his spiritlike soul *(hun)* rises upward. The *p'o* (Geddee's B-consciousness) dissolves but does not disappear; its "units" just separate but continue to exist as forces, as tendencies ready to take up a new becoming in the "soul of the land" or of the earth, which in psychological language means in the realm of the collective unconscious. A kind of spiritual consciousness, on the other hand, is attained in the *hun*. This, however, if it is without body, has a tendency to fade away gradually in a second death, unless the individual, during his lifetime, has concentrated so much on his future life that he has built a subtle body around himself, *a body of thoughts and deeds* (here again the fruit!) of a spiritual kind, which then supports the *hun* and protects it from dissociation. On the other hand, whoever has not built for himself such a spirit-body is dependent on an ancestor cult among his survivors to be able to continue to exist, in order to be incarnated anew among the same kin.

Jung observed a similar bipartition in people who faced immediate death. He comments in a letter on the strange change in a dying patient, a woman who seemed to linger on in an ecstasy:

> Such a thing is possible only when there is a detachment of the soul from the body. When that takes place and the patient lives

on, one can almost with certainty expect a certain deterioration of the character inasmuch as *the superior and most essential part of the soul has already left.*[26] Such an experience denotes a partial death. It is of course a most aggravating experience for the environment, as a person whose personality is so well known seems to lose it completely and shows nothing more than demoralization. . . . But it is the lower man that keeps on living with the body and who is nothing else but the life of the body.[27]

Jung's remark is similar to the Chinese description of the separation of the *hun* and *p'o* at death. He continues:

With old people or with persons seriously ill, it often happens that they have peculiar states of withdrawal or absent-mindedness, which they themselves cannot explain, but which are presumably conditions in which the detachment takes place. It is sometimes a process that lasts very long. What is happening in such conditions one rarely has a chance to explore, but it seems to me that it is as if such conditions had an inner consciousness[28] which is so remote from our matter-of-fact consciousness that it is almost impossible to retranslate its contents into the terms of our actual consciousness. I must say that I have had some experiences along that line. They have given me a very different idea about what death means.[29]

I have also observed such psychic states in some people. In these cases a second consciousness was often present, a superficial, everyday consciousness which seemed to have no notion of impending death and even made mundane future plans, and a deeper, more serious consciousness which broke through from time to time with casual remarks which made clear that the dying person was well aware of the impending end and was preparing himself for it.[30]

This "deeper consciousness" belongs presumably to the Self, which is partially out of time and space, and it is therefore that part of man which survives death.[31] The Chinese *p'o*, the body-bound life-force, maintains a kind of impersonal inheritance—one could also say it has "complexes"—which do not belong just to the individual.

Jung writes in a letter: "Our life is not made entirely by ourselves. The main bulk of it is brought into existence out of sources that are hidden to us. Even complexes can start a century or more before a man is born. There is something like karma." [32] The ancient Chinese expressed this insight in the following way: The body-soul elements of the vegetative *p'o* "are dispersed and are ready for a new existence." [33] They enter into the "soul of the land," a kind of life-reservoir from which the ancestors emerged and from which the grandchildren will arise again—that is, into the collective unconscious. "Chosen people, however, instead of falling into this dispersion are able to become a *shen*—an agent of divinity" [34]—and no longer have to return.

These are the people who through meditation have brought their entelechy to a continuous "circle of light." The famous taoistic-alchemical text, *The Secret of the Golden Flower*, refers to this great work. The analogy to Western alchemy and to the Egyptian cult of the dead is obvious. A spiritual opus is needed by man in order to produce a resurrection body (in Buddhism, the diamond body). First of all we must return to the duality of the *hun* and *p'o*. The task of the taoistic-alchemical opus, or of this kind of meditation, is not to suppress the thoughts of the *p'o*, which belong to the female yin principle, but rather to transform them into thoughts of the *hun* (yang). [35] These thoughts of the yin are "distinctive," discriminating. They have their source in a consciousness that has turned to the outer world; only after their transformation do they also become rooted in the creative, harmonious principle of the universe, in tao. Consciousness that has been transformed in this way is also referred to as a "holy embryo"; it is the dharma body, a form of higher consciousness. [36]

The *p'o* is that ego which still hopes, desires, wishes and experiences fear and thus lets the life energy *(ch'i)* flow outward. It corresponds to Geddee's B-consciousness or to an everyday ego that has not been purified. The work consists in its transformation into an interiorized, spiritual consciousness. This is the "fruit" which is being preserved after the destruction of the body in death, the "one grain of corn." [37]

Accordingly, therefore, this "body" which survives death would, in psychological terms, be made up of everything from the collective unconscious which the individual had, in life, brought into consciousness. That which our everyday ego thinks, does, feels, etc. throughout the day escapes into the outer world and finally gets lost there. But when something meaningful, which can be recognized by means of a strong emotion, breaks into our life, then there is a chance for us to make its archetypal (that is, spiritual) meaning conscious. In this way a piece of something eternal and infinite is realized in our earthly existence, and that means, in a literal sense, that it has become real.

So affects and emotions which belong to the body-soul should not be repressed and "overcome" (as some Christian teachings advise). One should confront them in oneself and search for the deeper meanings behind their exterior expressions of desiring and willing to act. Usually this confrontation does not end without a struggle, for it is in the nature of affects to seduce us into impulsive actions or to hold us tenaciously in the circumstances placed before us in the outer world. To concentrate instead on the deeper meaning of such impulses requires a conscious decision, a turning back or confrontation with one's own emotions. This, in the last analysis, is the meaning of the cross in Christianity, or of the crucifixion: complete endurance of the conflict between violent emotions and their spiritual meaning. This spiritual meaning, however, reveals itself only when one confronts the conflict without reservation. Then there occurs (one cannot make it happen) a transformation that leads to the union of the opposites, and out of that union, the glorified body apparently emerges that survives death and that the alchemists called their "stone."

# 9.

# Final Resurrection as a Reunion of the Psyche with the Body

*T*he principal part of the Komarios text continues as follows:

But when the dark, fetid spirit (pneuma) has been removed, so that no smell and no color of the darkness is perceptible any more, then the body is illuminated and soul, body and spirit rejoice that the darkness has retreated. And the soul calls back to the illuminated body: "Wake up from Hades and stand up from the grave and awaken from the darkness. For you have clothed yourself in spirituality and divinity. For the call of resurrection has sounded and the medicament of life *(pharmakon tes zoes)* has entered into you." Spirit and soul rejoice once again in the body which they now inhabit, and the soul, full of joy, hastens as quickly as possible to embrace the body and the soul embraces it. And the darkness no longer rules over it, for it has subordinated itself to the light and no longer permits itself to be separated from it in eternity, and it (the soul) rejoices in its house, because, after the body had been hidden in the darkness, (the spirit) found it full of light. And the soul united with the body, since the body had become divine through its relation to the soul, and it dwelt in the soul. For the body clothed itself in the light of divinity, and the darkness departed from it, and all were united in love, body, soul and spirit, and all became one; in this the mystery is hidden.

But the mystery was fulfilled in their coming together, and the house was sealed and the statue *(andrias)* was erected, filled with light and divinity. For the fire had made and transformed them into one, and it (the one) has come forth out of its womb. In the same way, it has come forth out of the womb of water and air, which serve them (the bodies), and it (the air)[1] has carried them out of the darkness into the light, from suffering to radiance, from weakness to health and from death to life. And they have clothed themselves with the divine spiritual glory *(doxa)*, which they did not have before, for therein lies the whole hidden mystery, for the divine cannot be changed. But as a result of their active nature, the bodies penetrate each other and, coming out of the earth, they clothe themselves with light and divine glory, in keeping with their nature. . . . And this glory carried them to a unique unity, and the statue (or the image: *eikon*) was completed, having body, soul and spirit, and they became one. For the fire was subordinated to the water and the earthly part[2] to the air. In the same way the air with the fire and the earth with the water and the water with the earth and with the air. They, too, became one. Plants and sooty smoke *(aithalon)* became one and nature and the divine elements became divine. Natures ruled over natures and conquered them and natures and bodies changed thereby . . . for the fugitive has penetrated the non-fugitive and the strong the weak and they have all become one.[3]

This passage is followed by other general remarks on the arrangement of the cosmos and the structure of the astrological "skypole." Then the text continues:

And now I tell you that the sky is set to the movements of the four elements and never remains silent. These (four elements) were planted in our Ethiopian earth, from which plants, stones and divine substances *(somata)* are taken, which God has planted (there) and not man. But the creator has implanted in each of them a power, in some a power to green, in others a power not to green, in some dryness, in others dampness, in some the power to remain fixed, in still others the power to separate, in some a power for possessing and in others for retreating. And in their encounters they conquer each other . . . and there is joy in the other which shines within it. And the one nature comes into being which pursues and rules over all natures, and this same one conquers every nature, namely fire and earth, and it transforms all their powers. And I tell you what the goal (of the one) is: when it is completed, it becomes a deadly medicine which circulates in the body. In the same way that it enters its own body, (so) does it also penetrate the (other) bodies. In putrefaction and warmth (there is created) a medicine which penetrates every body without hindrance.[4]

What appears to be important here is the fact that the reunion of soul and body is no longer a union of opposites, since the body is no longer body but has become psyche as well, but of

*Fig. 12:* The Ba-bird, encrusted with semi-precious stones, settles itself on the breast of the mummy. From this union of Ba-soul and Ka-soul emerges the "Ach," "this transfigured one."

the *one* nature. It is therefore the body-*soul* which is being assimilated and integrated, not the coarse material body. This idea also appears in Petrus Bonus, who, in his *Pretiosa margarita novella,* says:

> It was through their knowledge of the art that the old philosophers knew of the coming of the end of the world and the resurrection of the dead. Then the soul will be united with its original body for ever and ever. The body will become wholly transfigured (*glorificatum*), incorruptible, and from incredible luminosity and almost unbelievable subtility it will penetrate all solids. Its nature will be as much spiritual as corporeal.[5]

It is not possible to interpret in detail every sentence of the obscure, indifferently translated and partially damaged Komarios text. I have therefore selected only the more clearly formulated motifs. However, one theme should be clear, namely, how closely the production of the alchemical elixir (a synonym for the philosopher's stone) was, from the very beginning, associated with the motif of the resurrection of the dead.

What emerged at the end of the process was called, among other things, an *andrias,* a human-shaped statue—something solid and at the same time a deadly elixir which was actually a drug, a poison, a remedy that could penetrate all solids.

The process of resurrection as described in this part of the text consists of a reunion of *pneuma*, "spirit," *psyche* (soul) and the purged, deified or transfigured body. The relatively analogous motif in Egypt would be the union of the *ba* with the *ka* and the mummy. The result was referred to as "this transfigured one [Ach]." At first, the deified body was still relatively dead or immobile, until *ba* and *ka* were united with it.[6] Only then did the deceased become an *ach*, a transfigured one, and was once again full of life.

The *ba* was a freely moving, nonstationary part of a man's soul. It had the shape of a bird, thus emphasizing its spiritual nature, but it was also represented as a star or in the shape of a man.[7] In the hieroglyph for star, the *ba*'s affiliation with the heavenly sphere was emphaasized.

Helmut Jacobsohn says that the *ba* represents the still unconscious individuality of man, the innermost center of his being (the "basic ground of the soul," in the language of the Christian mystics). It reveals itself as an inner voice and is at the same time the quintessence of the natural inner man *and* a divine *coincidentia oppositorum*.[8] Unlike the *ba*, the *ka* (usually translated as "shadow") seems to have a greater connection with man's life force, potency, and skill. It is a kind of double image, which however usually lives within the body and "one captures him" after death, as it were, in the statue of the deceased. In Upper Nigeria and in the Volta region, similar ideas still exist today.[9]

In the Komarios text the result of the union is called *eikon* (picture). In the Greek world of ideas the concept of soul *(psyche)* was also many-sided and flexible.[10] For Homer, psyche and *eidolon* (image) were originally the same, and at death they went to Hades. In addition, there was also the *thymos*, which one could interpret as "life impulse." This was mortal.[11] The image *(eidolon)* was also understood as a kind of visible mask behind which hides the incomprehensible. According to Herodotus, the Greeks were influenced by the Egyptians in their view of the psyche as being immortal[12] (for instance, with Pindar and Plato); and with Aristotle the soul became an entelechy which constructs its own body. But it also contains the immortal *nous*—the soul of reason—which belongs more to the purely divine realm of existence. The Romans' idea of the *genius* went through a similar transformation. The *genius* was first understood as the mortal essence of the being or of the identity of the individual. Later, under Graeco-Egyptian influence, it was referred to as the entity which survives death.

In Egypt, as previously mentioned, the mummy was called an "image." The earth god Aker guards the "great image," but at the same time the mummy is a "mystery," because it is precisely on or in it that the transformation process begins anew. The *ka* —with the qualities the Romans attributed to the *genius*— remains close to the mummy or to a statue of the deceased, whereas the *ba* is also able to accompany the sun god in the upper world on his journey across the sky or joins the "never-setting" circumpolar stars. In the Komarios text, which is undoubtedly based on Egyptian ideas, pneuma, psyche and soma are once again united. Pneuma most probably refers to the *ba* and psyche to the *ka*. Admittedly, one should not take such "translations" too literally, for even with the Greeks and Egyptians themselves these terms were applied to vague and flexible concepts. The third element in the Komarios text is the purified body, clothed in glory *(doxa)*, which is the mummy after its reanimation through pneuma and psyche. This whole, newly animated corpse is also what the Egyptian texts often called the *ach*, the transfigured one.

Transfiguration is also described as the acquisition of a garment of light. In the Egyptian Book of Am-Tuat, Re says to the mummy gods in the eighth hour: "You are ornamented with your clothing, you are protected by your garments." And in the Book of Gates, the reanimated mummies are addressed: "Hail to you, Achu (transfigured, blessed dead) . . . hail to you, underworld ones. . . . May you shine through your (white!) garments, may you be bright in the brilliance of Re." In the Book of Caves, it is said that mummies are "dressed in the form of Osiris,"[13] in the same way that the Komarios text speaks of the body of the dead as being decorated "with divine glory" *(doxa)*.

This motif of the *doxa* seems to me to point not only to Egyptian tradition but even more to the influence of Persian ideas, possibly through the mediation of Gnostic sources. The *doxa* reminds one of the Persian *xvarnah* which comes to meet the newly deceased and which is variously called "light of glory," a "victory," a "victorious fire." In the Mithraic cult this light-glory also meant the fulfillment of individual fate. It illuminates the dead, along with his *daena*—his other-worldly anima.[14] This *imago gloriae* "envelops" the entire soul of the dying man, like a "shining illumination by a spiritual fire which inflames the soul to ardor"; it is at the same time the light of healing knowledge. This same image is to be found in the Gnostic Acts of Thomas.

After the reunion, continues the Komarios text, the house was sealed and "the statue was erected, filled with light and divinity." This probably refers to the end of the Egyptian burial ceremony, when the grave chamber is sealed and the so-called *djed* pillar is erected, along with the statue of the dead, in the *serdab*. The statue *(andrias)* is also called *eikon*, "image." It consists of the four elements that have been united as one and it is also a medicine (elixir) which penetrates everything and is, at the same time, something solid.

The homunculus-priest who, in the visions of Zosimos, first tears himself to pieces is transformed eventually into a "man of gold." The text continues:

> In short, my friend, build a temple from a single stone, like to white lead, to alabaster, to Proconnesian marble,[15] with neither end nor beginning in its construction. Let it have within it a spring of the purest water, sparkling like the sun. . . . A dragon lies at the entrance, guarding the temple. Lay hold upon him; immolate him first; strip him of his skin and, taking his flesh with the bones, separate the limbs; then, laying (the flesh of the limbs) together with the bones at the entrance of the temple, make a step of them, mount thereon, and enter, and you will find what you seek. The priest, that brazen man, whom you see seated in the spring and composing the substance, (look on) him not as the brazen man, for he has changed the colour of his nature and has become the silver man; and if you will, you will soon have him (as) the golden man.[16]

In the same text it is also said of the homunculus-priest that "he makes the eyes clairvoyant, and raises the dead."[17] The dismembering (and, in variants, the cooking) of the initial substance is also explicitly described as *taricheia* (mummification).[18] The sacrifice of the dragon is in some variants also a sacrifice of the priest himself. In the alchemical view, he represents the microcosmos or the *monas*, the initial matter, which also contains the goal of the work. His dismemberment signifies a new conscious ordering of his initial chaotic nature.[19]

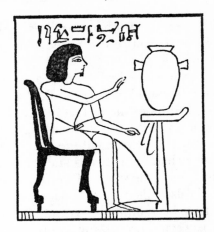

*Fig. 13:* The stone, an old Egyptian god-image, represented as a "Heart of Stone," and associated with the Benben-stone of Heliopolis and with the phoenix: "I am the phoenix *(Benu)*, the Ba of Re."

Important for us here is the monolithic temple, the temple built of a single stone, in which there springs a fountain of life, and "this is a hint that the production of the round wholeness, the stone, is a guarantee of vitality. Similarly, the light that shines within it can be understood as the illumination which wholeness brings. Enlightenment is an increase of consciousness."[20] The golden man sitting on the stone represents the inner man who has gradually become the highest value.[21]

The stone was already an important god symbol in the religion of ancient Egypt. In the sanctuary of the temple in Heliopolis (On), a mysterious divine stone called Benben was revered. Its name is connected with *w-b-n*, which means "to rise, to light up," especially in connection with the sun or the stars. The *b-n-w* bird is also formed from the same verbal stem. Both the name for the phoenix, the Benben stone and the *b-n-w* bird were looked upon as outward forms of Atum, the highest of the gods,[22] and the stone was also an image of the primal hill which first emerged from the primeval waters and signified the beginning of the world. The phoenix later became a symbol of the *ba. Benbenet* was later also the name for the apex of a pyramid, and even later the dead received a small *benbenet* stone as a burial offering. The dead king watched the sun set from the top of a pyramid, so the *benbenet* would seem to have a connection with resurrection or with an awakening of the dead to new consciousness. Jacobsohn has correctly pointed out an analogy between the Benben stone in Egypt and the alchemical "stone," both of which symbolize psychic totality and a *complexio oppositorum.*

What the stone might mean to the postmortal condition can also be seen in a vision which Jung reports in his memoirs. In a near-death experience he seemed to be floating over the earth from a height of "approximately a thousand miles!" As he gazed around him he saw "a tremendous dark block of stone, like a meteorite . . . floating in space." Near an entrance in the stone sat a black Hindu who seemed to expect him. "Tiny niches" with "small burning wicks surrounded the door."[23] Jung felt certain that he "was about to enter an illuminated room and would meet there all those people to whom (he belonged) in reality." There he would also understand what "historical nexus" his life fitted into. "I would know what had been before me, why I had come into being, and where my life was flowing."[24] At that moment he was called back to earth by the emerging image of his doctor.

The same stone, although in somewhat different form, appeared to Jung a second time a few days before his actual death. It was the last dream he was able to communicate:

> He saw a great round stone in a high place, a barren square, and on it were engraved the words: "And this shall be a sign unto you of Wholeness and Oneness." Then he saw many vessels to the right in an open square and a quadrangle of trees whose roots reached around the earth and enveloped him and among the roots golden threads were glittering.[25]

The image of the temple made of a single stone also provides illumination here, as it does in the Zosimos visions. And in the image of the stone in Jung's last dream, becoming whole is emphasized, as it is in the Komarios text.

Jung often remarked that it seemed to him that his individual ego life emerged like a rhizome (the underground root system of a plant, especially observable in mushrooms); he himself lived fleetingly above ground, but some kind of life lived on in the depths.

> Life has always seemed to me like a plant that lives on its rhizome. Its true life is invisible, hidden in the rhizome. The part that appears above ground lasts only a single summer. Then it withers away—an ephemeral apparition. When we think of the unending growth and decay of life and civilizations, we cannot escape the impression of absolute nullity. Yet I have never lost a sense of something that lives and endures underneath the eternal flux.[26]

In his last dream Jung returns to the rhizome—*without any dissolution of his individual form*, sheltered in the womb of the earth. The roots represent a spiritual process of development which lasts much longer than a human lifetime, "compared with which the individual is no more than the passing blossom and fruit of the rhizome."[27]

The vessels which surround Jung in the dream remind one of the Canopic jars in ancient Egyptian graves in which the entrails of the corpse, separated from the mummy, were preserved, and which had as lids the heads of the four sons of Osiris. According to the embalmment text, the four jars represent the limbs of the gods. Their "fat" or their "ointment" (psychic essence) penetrated the entrails of the corpse and "protected them," that is, rendered them imperishable.[28]

The motif of the stone also appears in the death experience of a man killed in the war, as reported by Hampe. In a state of unconsciousness, from which he awakened only briefly, he saw his mother and father, then wandered with them in the mountains through a blossoming landscape.

> I found a large stone and turned it over; it was weightless. On the back of it there was a large number of the most beautiful mountain crystals. They were arranged together to form something resembling a cathedral. I felt happy about it.[29]

In light of this amplification, the red stone that remained unblackened by fire in the dream given earlier takes on a fuller meaning. It is the symbol of that form of the dreamer's existence which will survive his impending death. In Jung's dream the stone appears as a temple, a much more differentiated image than those in the two other examples, probably because Jung was occupied, more than most people, with the Self, with his relationship to his inner totality.

We find the motif of an eternal house in the Beyond in many grave rituals. The Romans spoke of the grave as *domus aeterna*, a reflection back to Egyptian and ancient Oriental prefigurations. The graves were often completely and comfortably furnished and replete with household goods,[30] and there the deceased and his kin lived together forever. The Etruscans clearly marked the graves of women with a small house, those of men with a phallus.

The stupas of Buddhist cultures seem to have had a similar significance originally. As R. Mus has shown, they go back to ancient pre-Buddhistic burial customs in which the gravestone was supposed to represent "the world of the dead in miniature" and, at the same time, the universe in the form of *purusha* (primal man, cosmic man). Mus stresses that

> the tomb is not so much a dwelling place for the dead as it is a substitute for the former transitory mortal frame of the deceased. . . . It is therefore a constructed body which represents the abode of the dead in the same way that his physical body did when he was alive. Although the teaching emphasizes that Buddha is no longer here—having gone into nirvana— popular belief has imagined such an eternal body of Buddha in the stupas. A Japanese text even says quite simply: "The body of Buddha, seen from the outside, is a stupa." Or the stupa is at least that part of Buddha himself which, after the parinirvana, has remained in this world. Ghandaran art, which has been influenced by Western antique art, has also created illusionary images of Buddha's death, but it soon attempted once again to describe the non-reality of this death. Certain later teachings stated that after his death Buddha still possesses three bodies: the *dharma-kaya*, his true absolute being; the "body of beatification," through which he can still "be" somehow in nirvana; and thirdly, a shadow-body *(nirmana kaya)*, through which Buddha knowingly helps other beings to attain nirvana. Whoever sees this shadow-body of Buddha has actually had only a subjective experience.[31]

What is important for our consideration here is that the shrine, the stupa, was also looked upon as a substitute, stone body of the dead Buddha; the stupa, as we know, is a three-dimensional mandala.

Thus the stone can also, therefore, be a house or a grave-temple. In this connection, Jung had an impressive dream two months before his death:

> From an unknown place he had come to "his" Bollingen tower, which was all made of gold. He held the key to the tower in his hand "and a voice told him that the 'tower' was now completed and ready for habitation."[32] What was most impressive for him was the complete loneliness (no human being was around) and the absolute silence of the place. "Then far below he saw a mother wolverine teaching her child to dive and swim in a stretch of water,"[33] something which it could not yet do by itself.

After Jung had built his tower in Bollingen, he often had dreams in which an exact replica of the tower stood on the "other shore of the lake." He interpreted this to mean that his tower was actually just an earthly copy of its true form in the Beyond, i.e., the Self. His last dream of the tower says to him that now the other-worldly residence of the Self has been completed and is ready for him to move in. The animal motif at the end is a strange one. It conveys the idea that, as Mother Nature adapts and accustoms her children to life through their instincts, so an instinct will likewise help us to adapt to altered conditions in the Beyond.[34] For Jung, the tower, in its earthly form, was already a vessel of the greater inner man or of the Self. He writes about this in his memoirs:

> From the beginning I felt the Tower as in some way a place of maturation—a maternal womb or a maternal figure in which I could become what I was, what I am and will be. . . .
>
> At Bollingen I am in the midst of my true life, I am most deeply myself. . . .
>
> At times I feel as if I am spread out over the landscape and inside things, and am myself living in every tree, in the plashing of the waves, in the clouds and the animals that come and go.[35]

When Jung dreamed of the golden tower in the Beyond, the unconscious furnished him with a primal, eternal image, a copy of which he had built for himself on earth.

The white stone in the Zosimos text, which houses both the "golden man" and the life source, provides a parallel to Jung's dream. And the Eastern stupas seem to have a similar significance as a residence for the form of the Buddha which has remained on earth.

In the Komarios text the shining light of the unified nature of the "image," that is, its illuminating quality, is also emphasized. This unification, this resurrection of the deceased, this *andrias*, corresponds in the Zosimos vision to the brazen man who first becomes silver, then gold. In other words, it represents a kind of living metal statue.

The dream series published by Edinger includes the following dream:

> I was looking at a curiously unique and beautiful garden. It was a large square with a floor of stone. At intervals of about two feet were placed brass objects, standing upright, and looking very much like Brancusi's "Bird in Space." I stayed a long time. It had a very positive meaning but what that was I was unable to grasp.[36]

Edinger amplifies the image of the metal pole (Brancusi's "Bird in Space"), "thicker in its mid-region and tapering to a point at the top," as a "phallic, striving, vertical thrust upward towards the upper spirit realm." He cites as a parallel the Egyptian *djed* column, whose erection at the end of the burial ceremony signified resurrection. This column corresponds also to the phallus on the graves of Etruscan men. In a certain sense it could also be compared with the dancing flame of life in the dream of J. B. Priestley cited earlier—an image of the creative life impulse which lives on and on. In the above dream, this figure is made of bronze. Metal, as Jung points out,[37] has a strange, unfamiliar coldness, which characterizes this symbolic figure. Its sense of a far-away origin in the realm of inorganic matter conveys a foreignness which is also characteristic of the alchemical stone.

Many alchemists equated their stone with Christ, but as Jung has shown,[38] it had for them a closer relation to the human body. The stone was something divine which was presumed to lie hidden in cosmic matter. Insofar as Christ "became flesh," there exists an analogy to the *lapis;* but the latter is incarnated in *every* man and can be produced by *everyone.* That means that it can be made conscious inwardly. Thus the stone of alchemy does not really mean Christ but rather is a symbol that *compensates for* certain aspects of the figure of Christ. Jung writes:

> What unconscious nature was ultimately aiming at when she produced the image of the lapis can be seen most clearly in the notion that it originated in matter . . . and that its fabrication lay at least potentially within man's reach. These qualities all reveal what were felt to be the defects in the Christ image at that time: an air too rarified for human needs, too great a remoteness, a place left vacant in the human heart. Men felt the absence of the "inner" Christ who belonged to every man. Christ's spirituality was too high and man's naturalness was too low. In the image of Mercurius and the lapis the "flesh" glorified itself in its own way; it would not transform itself into spirit but, on the contrary, "fixed" the spirit in stone. . . . The lapis may therefore be understood as a symbol of the inner Christ, of God in man.[39]

The stone was considered to be the culmination of Christ's work of redemption. It came not from spiritual-metaphysical realms as the official Christ figure does, but "from those border regions of the psyche that open out into the mystery of cosmic matter."[40]

The Assumption of the Blessed Virgin is a dogma still in a state of flux, inasmuch as Mary ascended to heaven *with her body.* So this is only a beginning answer to a question which has not yet been solved in Christian teaching. It is a question, however, which troubles modern man. It seems to me to be high time that we occupy ourselves with the symbolism of alchemy, where it is also true that, admittedly, no final answer is to be found, but where an answer seems nevertheless to be hinted at symbolically.

I lost my father when I was relatively young and, about six weeks after his sudden death, I had the following dream:

> My father appeared to me, healthy, alive, but I knew in the dream that he was dead. He said to me in cheerful excitement, "The resurrection of the flesh is a reality. Come with me, I can show it to you." He started walking toward the cemetery where he was buried. I dreaded to follow him but I did. In the cemetery he walked around and between the graves, observing every one. Suddenly he pointed to a grave and called out, "Here, for instance, come and look." I saw that the earth there had begun to move and I stared in that direction, full of dread that a half-decomposed corpse was about to appear. Then I saw that a crucifix was drilling its way upwards out of the earth. It was about one meter long, golden-green and shining. My father called out, "Look here! *This* is the resurrection of the flesh."

In considering this dream, the expression "resurrected in Christ" naturally occurred to me, but what does this image really mean? It is a mystery that one cannot fathom. The essential image here seems to me to be the crucifix which was made of *animated metal*, like the statue in alchemy. The *green* gold as a motif alludes to alchemy. Jung reports in *Memories, Dreams, Reflections* that he once had a vision of a Christ figure made of green gold. He comments:

> The green gold is the living quality which the alchemists saw not only in man but also in inorganic matter. It is an expression of the life-spirit, the *anima mundi* or *filius macrocosmi*. . . . The emphasis on the metal, however, showed me the undisguised alchemical conception of Christ as a union of spiritually alive and physically dead matter.[41]

My dream emphasizes the same double nature of the resurrected body as a union of opposites. The cross, on the other hand, signifies the *suffering* which results from unreconciled opposites. My dream implies, furthermore, that the resurrected body is at the same time the eternal inner man, not the ephemeral ego, even though this ego—that of my dead father in the dream—seemed to have been retained as an observer of the process. Obviously man's complete wholeness is only attained with the union of the ego and the resurrected body.

An eighty-year-old woman dreamed, shortly before her death:

> She saw a cross; at the center stood a radiating sapphire. She knew in the dream she was experiencing a moment of heavenly existence.[42]

Here, too, the cross signifies the union of all opposites. In the medieval tradition the sapphire was considered to be the "foundation stone" of the Heavenly Jerusalem and an image of Christ.

# 10.
# The Subtle Body and Its Variants

*I*n many areas of the world, for instance in China and wherever Hinduism has spread, and also with many so-called primitives, the idea prevails that after death the soul —whatever that may be—possesses a kind of subtle body. Western spiritualism works with the same hypothesis and reports numerous materialization phenomena in which phantoms appear with a body formed of mist or smoke.[1] These are obviously manifestations of an archetypal idea; about the actual existence, however, of these phenomena, we have had almost no proof to date, apart from parapsychological reports. Jung drew our attention for the first time to a factor which might provide an empirically tangible hint for the possible existence of such a subtle body: the peculiar fact that *we have little conscious or direct information about what happens within our body.*[2] We know nothing, for instance, of the condition of our spleen unless a doctor provides some information, information which is only an inference drawn from indirect symptoms. This "gap," says Jung, seems to point to something lying between mind and body, perhaps to a subtle body which would exist interposed between the physical body and our perception of ourselves. One could perhaps develop Jung's suggestion further with a couple of reflections. The subtle-body layer is probably identical with the inwardly experienced, that is, with the introspectively perceived, psyche. We can all experience the way in which our emotions—jealousy, love, or hatred, certain intense thoughts, phantasy images, etc. —can confront the subjective ego quite objectively from within, that is, separated from the ego, so that one has the feeling that they rise up from within the body. In such instances, the subtle body would to some extent be identical with what Jung calls the "objective psyche"; or, from the other side, the objective psyche would sometimes possess a subtle-body aspect. Moreover, it is well known that during intensive states of excitement, as with a soldier in battle, one may be completely unaware of serious bodily injuries. The intensification of the psychic factor, i.e., the excitement, renders the body "unreal," and does this even though sense activities are heightened with the secretion of adrenalin that comes with excitement.

In light of Jung's reflections, it will be useful to take a closer look at the traditional theories concerning the existence of a subtle body. In antiquity, the Pythagorians, Orphics and Platonists taught that the soul possessed a kind of radiating subtle body as a vehicle *(ochema)* for its manifestation. According to Hierocles of Alexandria, the Pythagorian life principles served to free the soul from coarse matter and render it "bright" *(augoeides)* so that it would then be able to associate with the etheric beings (the gods).[3] In Plato's *Phaedrus* (250 C), the soul is described, before its descent into the grave, as "encompassed" in "brightness."

The expression "brightness" *(auge)*, used by Plato, later led the Neoplatonic commentators to refer to a "light soul" *(augoeides)*. It was specifically the Neoplatonists who developed the idea of the body of light or of a higher immortal subtle body. In a preserved fragment of Damascius we read: "The soul possesses a certain shining *(augoeides)* vehicle *(ochema)* which is also called 'star-like' *(asteroides)* and is eternal. It is situated in the body, either in the head or in the right shoulder."[4] In his commentary on Plato's *Parmenides*, Damascius describes this shining soul and remarks that when it incarnates itself it darkens more and more until it gradually becomes material, but in doing so does not lose its "number identity" (oneness?).[5] The radiant body and the light body of the soul do not blend abruptly into the coarse material body, according to the various authors; rather there still exists between body and soul a kind of "body spirit."[6] Through this the soul moves the body, makes the blood circulate, and causes the sense organs to function. This is a kind of quintessence of the four elements. When it is oriented upward, it produces rational, objective, psychic contents and ideas. If it is oriented downward it produces illusions *(phantasias)*. Then the soul becomes "wet" or "watery," as it were; whereas in its noble form it appears dry and fiery (Heraclitus!). Here we are again dealing with those flexible ego states as we have observed them in the cited modern material.

Plutarch (second century A.D.) describes the souls of the dead as follows: They are surrounded by a flamelike bubble or covering; some are of the purest full moonlight, sending out a soft, continuous color. Others are full of discolorations, covered with pale spots like vipers, others had slight scratches.[7] These discolorations are attributed to moral misdemeanors committed in the previous life. The late Neoplatonist Johannes Philoponus (seventh century) further differentiated the concept of the soul with the idea of a "pure soul part" that hastens away to the gods and that of an *eidolon*, a bodiless smoke or impure shadow which descends into Hades.[8] The purely rational, i.e., reasonable, soul is made of light and moves like a sphere; but when it abandons itself to foolishness and to the passions, it becomes obscure and moves in a straight line and then becomes cloudy and dark. Porphyry had already put forward similar views in his Platonic commentaries.[9] In the cloudy realm there are also demons who can influence the soul, whereas in its lucid pure state the soul is held apart from the demons. Phantoms *(phantasmata)* influence the soul as well and mold it to their form and color. Philoponus moreover proposed a fourfold partition in addition.[10] In his view man possesses (1) a rational soul that can be separated from the body and is immortal; (2) an irrational, passion soul that can be separated from the body but not from the rational soul; (3) a body spirit that survives the material body but does fade away after some time; and (4) a purely vegetative soul that vanishes immediately along with the material body. The body spirit goes to Hades, where, as we know from the Odyssey, it can be made to appear through a blood sacrifice on the part of its survivors. By means of a rigorous diet and steaming, it can be purified and made more volatile during its existence. Through the *imagination* of the spiritual soul also, it can be made to manifest itself.[11]

The early alchemists and hermetics were also acquainted with similar ideas of the time, and certain alchemists sought to produce in their work nothing less than a transformation and regeneration of the inner spirit of the subtle body. The most detailed account of this subject is in "The Visions of Zosimos."[12] Zosimos, who lived in Egypt (Panopolis), probably belonged to the Gnostic Poimandres sect.

Similar Neoplatonic ideas survived in the Islamic world as late as the eighteenth century, in that Shiite movement which is usually called Sheikism. One of its renowned representatives was Sheikh Ahmad Ahsa'i (died 1826), whose teaching Henri Corbin has described in detail.[13] Sheikh Ahmad, whose work deals essentially with the resurrected body, also proposes a fourfold partition of the soul, which however differs in some points from that of Philoponus. He distinguishes two *jasads*, "living organisms," and two *jism*(s), "body masses" or "body volumes." There is (1) *jasad* A, the ephemeral material body; (2) *jasad* B, which consists of subtle elements of the mystic earth Hurqalya and which Corbin equates with the *archetypus mundus*.[14] The *caro spiritualis*, the resurrection body, is composed of these two subtle elements; (3) *jism* A, a thing of the intermediary world which has its origin in the region of the sky and is thus a kind of astral body, ephemeral insofar as it is absorbed at the time of resurrection into *jasad* B, into the *caro spiritualis*, and therefore a kind of provisionary breath body; and (4) *jism* B, the essential subtle body, archetypal, eternal, imperishable, the eternal individuality, the *corpus supracoeleste* in man, his transcendental alter ego[15] and the light body.

For further deep and subtle interconnected associations with this conception of soul and body, I must refer to Corbin's basic work. In our context it is important that in such Neoplatonic, Hermetic, and alchemical ideas and those of certain Islamic mystics, soul and body are not seen as suddenly separated but are described rather as a partially continuous, only partially divisible multiplicity of regions. The previously mentioned plurality of souls, as imagined by numerous so-called primitives, shimmers through here, too. The alchemical tradition within this world of ideas is distinguished from the religio-philosophical tradition in that, between these aspects of the soul, the continuous element appears more emphasized. The work of the alchemists aims at making a *unity* of them, namely, by as great an incorporation as possible of the "layers" which are closer to the body.

Of the four psychosomatic components of man, as formulated by Sheikh Ahmad, we should look more closely at *jism* A (body volume), which is transient and is reabsorbed into *jism* B (eternal man) at the time of resurrection. It is a kind of astral body, insofar as it is the result of influences from the heavenly spheres. This idea of a smoke body composed of celestial influences also looks back to Neoplatonic and Gnostic views. Thus it was Plotinus' understanding that in its pure state the soul indeed possesses an ethereal body, but that when it passes from logos to imagination *(phantasia)* it receives a more sunlike body. When it descends even further it becomes more feminine and more bound to forms, and has a more moonlike shape, until finally it sinks down into the world of the body where it becomes quite amorphous, formed of moist vapors, overwhelmed by a complete unawareness of reality, by darkness and childishness. As soon, however, as it separates itself from this lower region, it becomes once again a shadowless and cloudless ray of light *(auge)*.[16]

Proclus formulates this somewhat differently in his commentary on Plato's *Timaeus*.[17] Man is a microcosm and like the universe *(to pan)* possesses mind and reason *(nous* and *logos)* and a divine as well as a mortal body. His mental nature corresponds to the fixed stars, the mind to Saturn, the social aspect to Jupiter. These are then followed by his unreasonable part, consisting of passions (Mars), eloquence (Mercury), desire (Venus), perception (sun), and the vegetative aspect (moon).

The radiating soul vehicle *(augoeides ochema)* corresponds to the sky, its mortal covering to the sublunary world. As Mead observes, in this respect Porphyry followed more the ancient Babylonian scheme, Proclus the new Babylonian.[18] According to Philoponus, the radiating soul vehicle consists, moreover, of the quintessence (the four coarse elements) whose form is spherical. And for Aristotle this quintessential body is transparent and crystal-like—an emanation of the heavenly spheres. With Philoponus this quintessential body corresponds to *jism* B, that is, to Sheikh Ahmad's resurrection body, which is formed out of the *mundus archetypus*, whereas the astral body resembles more the ephemeral *jism* A.

In the West, during the Renaissance, the alchemical tradition of the astral body was especially highly developed by Paracelsus. In the *Liber de lunaticis*, he states that "there are in man two bodies, one compounded of the elements, the other of the stars. . . . In death, the elemental body goes to the grave together with its spirit, but the ethereal bodies are consumed in the firmament."[19] Paracelsus refers here to the sidereal or astral body which indeed wanders around for some time after death as a mirror image or ghost, but is then gradually reabsorbed by the stars. Only "the spirit of the image of God goes to him whose image it is"[20]—that is, the immortal soul germ, psychologically the Self.

The astral body is thus looked upon sometimes by these writers as being transient, at other times as imperishable. Obviously

it is associated with what we would call the collective unconscious today. For since antiquity the celestial bodies have been
regarded as gods, in Islam as angels. Therefore, from the point
of view of modern man they are *archetypal symbols*, representing
in their entirety the collective unconscious. Consequently there
arises, in this connection, a great uncertainty: What happens to
the so-called collective unconscious in man at death? Does this
soul layer survive with him or does man separate from it, since it
has never really been a part of his personality or become a part of
his consciousness? Or is a part of it (according to Proclus, that
point which is situated above the moon) preserved together with
the "light body" and another part (the sublunary) cast aside? Or
does the cosmic aspect of the collective unconscious continue to
exist, separated from the deceased, while there remains with him
only that aspect which had been incarnated in him? Sheikh
Ahmad seems to incline toward the latter point of view. This is
why—to further interpret Corbin's reflections psychologically—
I would like to consider once again his idea more closely.

Ahmad believes (following Avicenna's cosmology) in an
"earth" which is situated between the upper realm of the intelli-
gible (of the pure mind of Platonic ideas) and the coarse material
earth. In it live the souls and certain angels. Its dimension is not
that of the world of the senses but of "active Imagination," that
is, an imagination which perceives and gives shape to that which
is psychologically objective and true, contrary to hallucinatory
wish-fulfillment dreams and illusions. It corresponds, as Corbin
notes, to the *imaginatio vera* of the alchemists, in contradistinction to the *imaginatio phantastica*. This "true Imagination"
is the origin of all religious experience, of visions, charismata,
revelations, true insights, etc. This realm, which is that of the
earth Hurqalya, which is the center of the whole world,
mediates between the realm of pure spirit and that of coarse matter. It is a *coincidentia oppositorum*, a region where the soul and
body meet indistinguishably in the center.

In the language of depth psychology, this "earth," as Corbin
recognizes, is indeed a *mundus archetypus*, but, one should add, it
is the *mundus archetypus which has been united with the archetype of the
Self*. Jung, following the Occidental tradition, calls this union the
*unus mundus* and has described it as the background of synchronistic events in the coarse material realm.[21] In a letter to Pastor

Fritz Pfäfflin, Jung refers to such a subtle-body world or earth in the Beyond. Pfäfflin had written to Jung that he had distinctly felt the presence of his brother—who had died in Africa in an accident—and had had a conversation with him. Jung replied:

> Now with regard to the exceedingly interesting conversation you had *post mortem* with your brother, it has all the characteristic features of these experiences. For one thing, there is the peculiar preoccupation of the dead with the psychic states of other (dead) persons. For another, the existence of (psychic) shrines or places of healing. I have long thought that religious institutions, churches, monasteries, temples, etc. as well as rites and psychotherapeutic attempts at healing were modelled on (transcendental) postmortal psychic states—a real *Ecclesia Spiritualis* as the prototype of the *Una Sancta* upon earth. In the East these ideas would be by no means unheard-of; Buddhist philosophy, for instance, has coined the concept of *Sambhoga-Kaya* for this psychic existence, namely *the world of subtle forms* which are to *Nirmana-Kaya* as the breath-body (subtle body) is to the material body. The breath-world is thought of as an intermediate state between *Nirmana-Kaya* and *Dharma-Kaya*. In *Dharma-Kaya*, which symbolizes the highest state, the separation of forms is dissolved into absolute unity and formlessness. [22]

In the same letter, Jung also suggest that in the deepest layers of the unconscious, which seem to be spaceless and timeless, there prevails "a relative eternality and a relative nonseparation from other psyches, or a oneness with them." [23]

This sphere is obviously identical with the Hurqalya earth of Islamic mysticism. Contact with this world of the *unus mundus* is vital for man. The entire process which today we call individuation is in its service.

Now we better understand what Jung writes in his memoirs:

> The decisive question for man is: Is he related to something infinite or not? That is the telling question of his life. Only if we know that the thing which truly matters is the infinite can we avoid fixing our interest upon futilities, and upon all kinds of goals which are not of real importance. Thus we demand that the world grant us recognition for qualities which we regard as personal possessions. . . . The more a man lays

> stress on false possessions, and the less sensitivity he has for what is essential, the less satisfying is his life. . . . If we understand and feel that here in this life we already have a link with the infinite, desires and attitudes change. In the final analysis, we count for something only because of the essential we embody, and if we do not embody that, life is wasted. . . .
>
> The feeling for the infinite, however, can be attained only if we are bounded to the utmost. The greatest limitation for man is the "self"; it is manifested in the experience: "I am *only* that:" Only consciousness of our narrow confinement in the self forms the link to the limitlessness of the unconscious.[24]

In this sense, the infinite, the unconscious, has a meaning only when it is linked to consciousness, otherwise it is, as it were, "lost in itself." It seems that only that part of it which one has made conscious does one take with him as "fruit," into the Beyond. This fruit seems to have a positive long-lasting influence in the "treasure house" or in the "library" or in the "grain barn" of the Beyond.

The same motif can also be seen in the application of astrological ideas. Astrological constellations represent the collective unconscious. They are images of the archetypes projected onto the sky. The natal horoscope presents a special, individual combination of archetypal—i.e., collective—elements, similar to the collective character of biological hereditary factors; but in the individual they take on an individual combination. The combination of stars in the horoscope makes clear, to a large extent, the individual being and also his psychic fate. Similarly, we know from experience that we can by no means make conscious or integrate any archetype *per se* in its entirety.[25] We can make conscious only that which offers itself to us from outside as a fated event, or from inside in the course of our life, and apparently, as stated, only *that* remains with us in death. But the act of making something conscious depends finally on the connection of the ego with the infinite or with something divine. To succumb to, or to be possessed by, an archetype can happen to anyone. Psychically, *nothing* is accomplished thereby. The demon simply comes and goes again. Only a conscious realization of the Self—which, as *spiritus rector* of all biological and psychological occurrences, represents the eventual unity of all archetypes—seems to represent a possession which cannot be lost, even in death.

In a letter to a woman mourning for a child who had died very young, Jung wrote:

> What happens after death is so unspeakably glorious that our imagination and our feelings do not suffice to form even an approximate conception of it. A few days before my sister died her face wore an expression of such inhuman sublimity that I was profoundly frightened.
>
> A child, too, enters into this sublimity, and there detaches himself from this world and his manifold individuations more quickly than the aged. So easily does he become what *you* also are that he apparently vanishes. Sooner or later all the dead become what we also are. But in this reality we know little or nothing about that mode of being, and what shall we still know of this earth after death? The dissolution of our timebound form in eternity brings no loss of meaning. Rather does the little finger know itself a member of the hand.[26]

With the sentence, "Sooner or later all the dead become what we also are," Jung alludes to the mystery of the Self in which all souls, those of the dead and of the living, are merged into a multiple unity. And this is similar to the teaching of the sages of India, who have always emphasized the unity of the personal Atman (Self) with the cosmic Atman.

# 11.
# Jung's New Hypothesis

*I*f we take the hypothesis of the existence of a subtle body seriously, then this would suggest that the transformation of the coarse material body (and its energic manifestation) would continue gradually into the psyche. This would mean that what we call physical energy and psychic energy today could, in the last analysis, be two aspects of one and the same energy. Jung formulated this hypothesis in the letter to Raymond Smythies in which he suggested the existence of a subtle body. After this proposal, Jung continued:

> It might be that the psyche should be understood as *unextended intensity* and not as a body moving with time. One might assume the psyche gradually rising from minute extensity to infinite intensity, transcending for instance the velocity of light and thus irrealizing the body. . . .
> . . . In the light of this view the brain might be a transformer station, in which the relative infinite tension of intensity of the psyche proper is transformed into perceptible frequencies or "extensions."[1] Conversely, the fading of introspective perception of the body explains itself as due to a gradual "psychification," i.e., intensification at the expense of extension. Psyche = highest intensity in the smallest space.[2]

We would therefore be dealing here with a form of energy which *gradually* changes, from the physically measurable to the psychically immeasurable. The subtle body in this sense would then be a form of the psyche that would indeed remain close to the body but would also still possess a certain minimal mass and extension in time-space, a form of appearance which admittedly would no longer be understood as physical in the ordinary sense of the word.

In any case, one must keep in mind, in this connection, that modern physics has, to a large extent, resolved our idea of material reality. Fritjof Capra, for instance, writes:

> In modern physics, mass is no longer associated with a material substance, and hence particles are not seen as consisting of any basic "stuff," but as bundles of energy. . . . The particles must

not be pictured as static three-dimensional objects, like billiard balls or grains of sand, but rather as four-dimensional entities in space-time. Their forms have to be understood dynamically, as forms in space and time. Subatomic particles are dynamic patterns which have a space aspect and a time aspect. Their space aspect makes them appear as objects with a certain mass, their time aspect as processes involving the equivalent energy.[3]

If we understand "matter" in this way, then the idea of a body passing into an intensity, a concentration of energy no longer extending in space and time would not be unthinkable. In a letter in which he comments on Stewart Edward White's *The Unobstructed Universe*, Jung also writes:

> The best idea in *The Unobstructed Universe* is perhaps that of frequency. It is an idea that dawned on me too during my attempts to explain the relative reality of metapsychic phenomena. The parallel White draws with the nature of thought seems to me to hit the mark very aptly. Thought has no quality in common with the physical world except its intensity, which in mathematical terms may be considered as frequency. You observe a distinct heightening of this intensity or frequency in all cases where either an archetype manifests itself or, owing to an absolute *abaissement du niveau mental*, the unconscious comes actively into the foreground as in visions of the future, ecstasies, apparitions of the dying, etc.[4]

Jung's hypothesis of a unity of physical and psychic energies seems so important to me that it would be worthwhile to review the symbolism of the dreams we have already considered in order to find out whether there are any hints which would support or contradict this idea.

First of all we have Priestley's dream of a life-flame running through a series of living and dead birds. An important detail in that dream is the increasingly *faster flowing of time*. This would correspond precisely with that increase in intensity about which Jung speaks. The white flame would then be an image for a psychic life of enormous tension which continues, as it were, through all of the coarse material appearances. The entire life process culminates in this white flame, which here literally "irrealizes" the life of the body, as Jung expresses it. As time keeps running faster, that is, as the flow of energy becomes more intensive, time appears to the observer to be virtually at a standstill. This is portrayed in the dream when the separate birds can no longer be distinguished in the movement. Everything seems to be spread out simultaneously within an endless space. The "smallest space" of psychic intensity would therefore be no less a point than the universe itself—perhaps a kind of *omnipresent point*, a well-known image for God in medieval philosophy.

The image of light appears more often than any other image in our quoted material. Jung has expressed the assumption that psychic reality might lie on a supraluminous level of frequency, that is, it could exceed the speed of light. "Light," in this case, would appropriately enough be the last transitional phenomenon of the process of becoming unobservable, before the psyche fully "irrealizes" the body, as Jung puts it, and its first appearance after it incarnates itself in the space-time continuum by shifting its energy to a lower gear. In addition to Moody's witnesses cited earlier, one also finds with him, and especially in the familiar parapsychological literature, numerous reports of such light phenomena accompanying death or connected with ghosts. A dream reported by John Sanford illustrates Jung's hypothesis most graphically. It is the dream of a Protestant clergyman, dreamed a few days before his death:

> . . . he sees the clock on the mantlepiece; the hands have been moving, but now they stop; as they stop, a window opens behind the mantlepiece clock and a bright light shines through. The opening widens into a door and the light becomes a brilliant path. He walks out on the path of light and disappears.[5]

The alchemist Gerhard Dorn describes such a window as a *fenestra aeternitatis* (window into eternity) or *spiraculum aeternitatis* (spiracle of eternity), a window or spiracle which opens itself for the adept as a result of his dedication to his opus, so that, in Jung's words, he may "escape from the stifling grip of a one-sided view of the world."[6]

In the language of Christian theology, Mary is praised as *fenestra evasionis*, the window which provides an escape from the world.[7]

Of the many impressive examples in Hampe's volume, there is

room here for only a few. The following comes from the architect Stefan von Jankovich:

> One of the greatest discoveries I made during death . . . was the oscillation principle. . . . Since that time "God" represents, for me, a source of primal energy, inexhaustible and timeless, continually radiating energy, absorbing energy and constantly pulsating. . . . Different worlds are formed from different oscillations; the frequencies determine the differences . . . Therefore it is possible for different worlds to exist simultaneously in the same place, since the oscillations that do not correspond with each other also do not influence themselves. . . . Thus birth and death can be understood as events in which, from one oscillation frequency and therefore from one world, we come into another.[8]

Jankovich comes very close here to Jung's view.

In the majority of accounts of such experiences of individuals near death, the subject has had distinct feelings of reluctance to return to everyday reality. This would be that moment when the brain begins to "grade down" from psychic intensity; it confines the individual once again to the necessary realities of space-time and mass. The body, which had been "irrealized," can once again be felt.

The account of Victor Solov—who was considered to have been clinically dead for twenty-three minutes—is less influenced by subsequent reflections, and in this sense more genuine than that of Jankovich:

> I was moving very quickly toward a bright shining net which vibrated with a remarkable cold energy at the intersecting points of its radiant strands. The net was like a lattice which I did not want to break through. For a brief moment my forward movement seemed to slow down, but then I was *in* the lattice. As I came in touch with it, the light flickering increased to such an intensity that it consumed and, at the same time, transformed me. I felt no pain. The feeling was neither agreeable nor disagreeable, but it filled me completely. From then on everything was different—this can be described only very incompletely. *The whole thing was like a transformer, an energy-transformer, which transported me into a formlessness beyond time and*

*space.* I was not in another place—for spatial dimensions had been abolished—but rather in another state of being.[9]

A similar lattice was also seen by one of Lindley's witnesses. The patient reported that the more he concentrated on the source of light, the more he realized how very strange it was. It was more than light, it was "a grid of power."[10] It looked to him like an Indian Summer spider web.

This lattice or net reminds one of the "curtain of threads" through which a woman dreamer saw her uncle disappear. The uncle had died at the time of the dream, although the woman had not yet received any information about his demise.[11]

I had the following dream five years after my father's death:

> I was with my sister and we both wanted to take Tram No. 8 at a certain place in Zurich, to go to the center of town. We leaped onto the tram and discovered too late that it was going in the opposite direction. I said to my sister, "If one of us had done this it would be just a mistake, but since both of us have done it, then there must be a meaning in it. Let's watch out for what it may lead to." Then there came a so-called "controlleur," who checked the tickets. On his cap were the letters "EWZ," which stands for Electricity Works of Zurich. I wondered why such a man would be the controlleur. At the next tram stop we got off and there a taxi drove up near us and out of it—came my father! I knew it was his ghost. When I started to greet him he made a sign not to come too near to him and then walked away to the house where he had lived. I called after him, "We don't live there any more." But he shook his head and murmured, "That doesn't matter to me now."

The important motifs in this dream are Tram No. 8 and the strange "controlleur." In number symbolism, eight represents timelessness and eternity. According to St. Augustine, after the seven days of creation came the eighth, "which has no more evening" (Sermon IX, 6). In alchemy eight is the number of completion.[12] With "controlleur" I associated the word "control." As is well known, the control in spiritualistic séances is a phantom person who mediates between the medium and the "spirits." Many mediums cannot work without such a control. He is, so to speak, her personified animus (with a male medium, his anima).

But why in my dream is there a workman from the Electricity Works of Zurich? My associations indicated that he might have something to do with the transformation of tension or of a frequency of current, presumably with a heightening of that frequency. All of these experiences seem to support Jung's hypothesis.

At a certain threshold in the increase of frequency, the psychic functions which produce our perception of time and space seem to cease functioning. Jung never got tired of stressing the fact that a certain part of the psyche is not bound to the space-time category. On this subject he writes, in a letter:

> What is commonly understood by "psyche" is certainly an ephemeral phenomenon if it is taken to mean the ordinary facts of consciousness. But in the deeper layers of the psyche which we call the unconscious there are things that cast doubt on the indispensable categories of our conscious world, namely time and space.[13] The existence of telepathy in time and space is still denied only by positive ignoramuses. It is clear that timeless and spaceless perceptions are possible only because the perceiving psyche is similarly constituted. Timelessness and spacelessness must therefore be somehow inherent in its nature, and this in itself permits us to doubt the exclusive temporality of the soul, or if you prefer, makes time and space appear doubtful. . . . It is sufficiently clear that timelessness and spacelessness can never be grasped through the medium of our intelligence, so we must rest content with the borderline concept. Nevertheless we know that a door exists to a quite different order of things from the one we encounter in our empirical world of consciousness.[14]

And in another letter:

> The point is that, like all our concepts, time and space are not axiomatic but are statistical truths. This is proved by the fact that the psyche does not fit entirely into these categories. It is capable of telepathic and precognitive perceptions. To that extent it exists in a continuum outside time and space. We may therefore expect postmortal phenomena to occur which must be regarded as authentic. Nothing can be ascertained about existence outside time. The comparative rarity of such phenomena suggests at all events that the forms of existence inside

and outside time are so sharply divided that crossing this boundary presents the greatest difficulties. But this does not exclude the possibility that there is an existence outside time which runs parallel with existence inside time. Yes, we ourselves may simultaneously exist in both worlds, and occasionally we do have intimations of a twofold existence. But what is outside time is, according to our understanding, outside change. It possesses relative eternity.[15]

Jung's time hypothesis is well illustrated in the following conversation with a dying woman, as reported by Lückel. Lückel said to her that he had the impression that she lived in two different kinds of time.

> "Yes, exactly," she replied. "This is a very beautiful feeling, on the one hand, but also a very strange one. One time runs, the other stands still. And I can even influence it myself—a little bit anyway." Lückel: "Then these indeed are two quite different feelings in you, two simultaneous but different time-feelings." She: "Yes. One feeling is quite far away and deep, *as if I could be everywhere at the same time.* So I feel as if my body were somehow like air, or rather like light—as if there were no limits. . . . The other feeling is as if someone counts my moments. This goes on and on. I can't stop it. It is as if I am becoming less and less."[16]

It is obviously not only our experience of space and time that ceases at the threshold of death but also the connection between the psyche and brain activity. As a result the psyche is no longer extensity, but only intensity. Perhaps this is what is suggested by all those experiences of light, since light is still virtually the highest perceivable limit of extensity.

Jaffé reports that the light motif appears with great frequency. The following are just a few examples.

A woman reported having seen, on Christmas Eve, her dead father coming toward her, "shining and lovely as gold, and transparent as mist."[17] Others report seeing the dead as "transparent and bright as the sun,"[18] or as "appearing in a religious light."[19] Or the light appeared shortly before the figure of the dead person entered.[20] It is described variously as "unusual brightness," as "remarkable glow," or as "dazzlingly bright like the sun." These are appearances seen in dreams or waking visions. Wicked ghost figures also often appear in such a light. Thus a man who is riding in his carriage through the forest at a place which is supposed to be haunted by a child murderess sees a strong, even excessively bright, beam or sphere of light from which the horses flee in panic. Another sees, on the street at the scene of a suicide, a glaring cone of light with two figures inside. Admittedly, such light manifestations can also appear when an autonomous complex of a living person is intensively constellated.

I find the red light which flashes out of the black night chest in the dream cited earlier on especially significant. The black rectangle as coffin or grave must surely be associated with death, and out of it come the flashes. This reminds one of Origen's strange idea that the resurrected body emerges from the corpse through a kind of *spintherismos* (emission of sparks), as if energy were flowing out of the dead body in order to form a resurrected one. This may also suggest a gradual connection between the physically "material" body and the postmortal form of existence.

We find even more symbolism of the subtle body, of light and energy intensity in Mattiesen's material concerning the appearance of phantoms at the death bed.[21] Thus, at the bedside of a Horace Frankel, witnesses saw the phantom of his friend Walt Whitman taking shape as a "small cloud" which then became the figure of Whitman. When a witness touched it, he felt "a kind of light electrical vibration."[22] Von Güldenstubbe describes a similar appearance. One evening he saw "a dark column of grey vapor," which gradually became blue, then turned into the figure of a man. As the phantom dematerialized, it changed back again into a column, "the light fading quite gradually, flickering for a while like a lamp which is dying out."[23]

Mediums describe materializations as substances formed of a "low number of vibrations."[24] Mattiesen also discusses some theories of mediums, which, however, seem to me to be too speculative. On the other hand, it does seem probable that his suggestion that the coldness, the cold wind, and the smoke which accompanies the appearance of spirits may be accounted for by the fact that apparitions take energy away from the living (in order to make themselves visible).[25] At any rate the symbolism in such parapsychological reports suggests energic processes.

The following impressive dream was dreamed three days before the death of a Mr. C. by a woman friend of his:

> I am in an extremely high position where I become aware of a tremendous *intensity* of some kind. I could not tell whether it was heat or cold. I knew Mr. C. had died and then I caught sight of him on a small shining cloud with two other figures dressed in white, like serving angels or cherubs.

The metal box in the dream cited earlier also indicates a radiating energy. The dreamer associated the urn holding the ashes of her dead son with a container filled with a radioactive substance that could radiate throughout the entire universe. This dream hint could be seen as an expression of Jung's hypothesis of a supraluminal form of energy or a form of existence of the non-incarnated psyche.

Some of the hypotheses of contemporary physicists agree with such an energic view, for physicists today in general tend to regard the entire material universe as a "cosmic dance of energy."[26] The physicist David Bohm comes especially close to Jung's idea, for he also reflects on the possibility of nonobservable aspects of existence.[27] Bohm accepts, first of all, the hypothesis of an indivisibility of all material processes, a principle which was contested in the so-called paradox of Einstein, Podolsky, and Rosen.[28] To illustrate this paradox a hypothetical experiment was suggested in which two particles (A, B), once bound together in a system whose disintegration does not influence the spin of either particle, are observed as totally separated. However, a disturbance of the spin in A causes a corresponding disturbance in B, whereby an interaction of even a light signal becomes impossible. It is as if B "knows" what happens to A.[29] This implies that it is possible that, at its lowest level, the universe is *an indivisible whole*. Bohm postulates moreover that the observable material universe is just the unfolded or "explicate order" of existence as the surface of an underlying enfolded or "implicate order."[30] Both "orders" coexist in an indefinable holomovement, that is, in an "undivided wholeness." Explicate and implicate ensembles exist continuously, locked together in the incomprehensible totality of movement.[31]

The manifest world, which can be comprehended with our

senses, is the explicate world; it is the world our consciousness perceives, or which is actualized through conscious observation. "Matter in general and consciousness in particular may, at least in a certain sense, have this explicate (manifest) order in common,"[32] and both are based on an implicate order of higher dimensions. "Thus . . . *what is* is movement which is represented in thought as the co-presence of many phases of the implicate order."[33]

For the psychologist it is clear that in his idea of an "implicate order" David Bohm has outlined a projected model of the collective unconscious,[34] so that in his theory we have before us an attempt to outline a psychophysical model of the unity of all existence. The background of this existence, as Bohm expresses it, is an infinite reservoir—a "vast 'sea' "—of energy[35] which lies deeply behind/under our consciousness, which is unfolded in space-time.

This new image of the physical world can very well be associated with Jung's hypothesis of a single energy, which physically appears to be unfolded in space-time, but coexists psychically as pure spaceless-timeless (enfolded) intensity.

Other modern physicists also venture to propose such speculative outlines of a unified psychophysical world image. Fritjof Capra has compared the contemporary concept of matter as an "energy dance" with Far Eastern ideas of the tao and of the dance of Shiva,[36] and Olivier Costa de Beauregard concludes, on the basis of the problems of the information theory, "that the universe investigated by the physicists is not the whole, but it provides us with an idea of the existence of another *psychic* universe, of which the material universe represents only a passive and partial double."[37] The psychic universe is timeless, is spread throughout space and also contains a transpersonal knowledge, a knowledge which Jung ascribes to the collective unconscious. Jean Charon postulates a psychic omniscience for some electrons.[38] Naturally these are all speculations which still cannot be regarded today as certainties, but one recognizes in them a tendency towards a supposition that there could be something of a psychic and material world background in which cosmic matter and the collective unconscious would be two aspects of one and the same world foundation.[39]

Perhaps the various staircases, ladders, etc., which appear so often in the cited dream material, also point to a more *gradual* connection between the two forms of energy (body matter and psyche). At the same time there occurs at death perhaps a gradual liberation from the bonds of space-time, and seen thus it would not be surprising that it is especially in the vicinity of places where death has occurred that synchronistic phenomena occur most frequently. In the light of Jung's hypothesis, this whole complex of questions is thus fused together into an astonishing unity.

The hypothesis of a gradual connection between the physical body and the nonincarnated psyche is not refuted by the fact that the onset of death appears to be relatively abrupt. (We know, however, that medically it is not at all easy to specify the exact moment of death.) We can observe that in numerous energic processes there are "thresholds" where relatively "sudden" changes occur: for instance at the freezing point or at the beginning of the evaporation of a liquid. In the material presented in this volume there are numerous hints of the existence of such a "threshold."[40] An example is the earlier cited dream of the dying candle which then continues to burn brightly outside the window. The threshold here is symbolized by solid glass, a strong isolating substance. It seems as though the candle dematerializes and then materializes again on the other side of the window, for on the one side it was burned out but on the other is of normal size again and goes on burning. Another example is the lattice in Solov's near-death experience. This also seems to represent such a threshold. The fact that such thresholds exist in nature is best illustrated by the so-called "black holes" recently discovered in outer space. Stars of a certain order of magnitude presumably become denser and denser due to the mutual gravitational attraction between its particles; as is well known this gravity increases quadratically with a decreasing distance between particles. This results in a collapse of gravity. The space-time around the star becomes more and more curved until finally not even light can escape from it; it "sucks up" all light beams that come near it. Thus an "event horizon" is formed around the star, within which nothing can any longer be observed. The star moves out of our time, as it were, and disappears from our observation, although "it is still there."[41]

Something similar is symbolically hinted at in the following dream of an analysand of mine, who had only a few hours with me. She did not know Jung personally but venerated him from afar. The night after his death, of which she knew nothing, she dreamed:

> She was at a garden party where many people were standing around on a lawn. Jung was among them. He was wearing a strange outfit: in front his jacket and trousers were bright green, in the back they were black. Then she saw a black wall which had a hole cut out of it in exactly the same shape as Jung's stature. Jung suddenly stepped into this hole, and now all that one could see was a complete black surface, although everyone knew that he was still there. Then the dreamer looked at herself and discovered that she, too, was wearing such clothes, green in front and black behind.

She awakened very puzzled by the dream, then heard a radio report that Jung had died. This dream seems to me to want to say that death is a problem of a threshold of perception between the living and the dead. The latter have disappeared behind an "event horizon," as it were, like stars in a black hole, but they are still in existence. Many black Africans put considerable stress on the unity of the Here (life) and the There (the realm of the dead).[42] An old Zulu woman explained this in the following way. She held out her hand with the palm turned upward and said, "That's how we live." She then turned her hand over with the palm downward and said, "That's how the ancestors live."[43] One could not express more clearly the idea that the worlds of the living and the dead together form a whole. In a similar manner, Jung writes in a letter:

> This spectacle of old age would be unendurable did we not know that our psyche reaches into a region held captive neither by change in time nor by limitation of place. In that form of being our birth is a death and our death a birth. The scales of the whole hang balanced.[44]

# 12.
# Summary

*A*ll of the dreams of people who are facing death indicate that the unconscious, that is, our instinct world, prepares consciousness not for a definite end but for a profound transformation and for a kind of continuation of the life process which, however, is unimaginable to everyday consciousness.

Symbols which appear in the dreams present a thematic or structural harmony with the teachings of the various religions about life after death. We have seen, moreover, that they employ a great number of mythical images. I have presented only a relatively small number of cases in this study, but I entertain the hope that they might stimulate some teamwork on a large-scale systematic study. This, of course, would require experts, not only with psychological understanding, but also with a wide ethnological and religio-historical knowledge. I believe that such a project would produce even more surprising results.

This study answers only a few questions; it raises anew many old ones and suggests many new ones.

Does survival after death—if it exists—continue for only a limited period of time or longer? How do the dead relate to each other? What is meant by a timeless existence? Why are there both tragic and blissful images of the Beyond which do not take into account the culture-specific, moral evaluations of the various religions? Does the personality of the deceased disintegrate, and, if so, is this always so or only in certain cases? What does partial dying, as mentioned by Jung, mean? Are there any traces of the reincarnation hypothesis? Etc., etc.

The great uncertainty about death, which is felt consciously or unconsciously by a great many people today, remains with us. One can only envy those who can look forward to death while being firmly anchored in some belief.

Edinger calls the series of dreams in *Ego and Archetype* "metaphysical" dreams. They are indeed different from the majority of dreams we work with in psychotherapeutic practice. Somehow they cannot be interpreted very well on the subjective level, that is, as symbolic representations of subjective inner processes. This means that they cannot, in Jung's terminology, be "psychologized." One feels compelled to leave them in space as a symbolic statement about another reality from which we are separated by a mysterious and dangerous barrier. The fact that we discover this in the human psyche today seems to me to have some relevance to the fact that modern physics has also begun to speak about universes "with which we cannot communicate." We stand at a great turning point in modern science, which points toward the healing discovery that we are everywhere surrounded by rationally impenetrable mysteries. This is a recognition that hopefully signifies the beginning of a period of greater intellectual modesty. For me, however, this does not mean a turning away from questions or from further research. Perhaps some readers may have noticed that, throughout this work, the scientific investigation of dreams based on the discoveries of C. G. Jung is able to bring to light many more illuminating realities. These would also, perhaps, raise new, pressing, and difficult questions.

# Notes

INTRODUCTION

1. I would like to thank most heartily my young friend Emmanuel Xipolitas Kennedy, who has provided me with a broad overall view of the existing literature, something I could not have managed without his help. Moreover, he also made available his unpublished dissertation, *Archetypische Erfahrungen in der Nähe des Todes*.

2. *Death, the Final Stage of Growth*. See also *Living with Death and Dying*.

3. This was an early, erroneous interpretation of Freud's, which, after a closer examination of dreams, cannot be sustained.

4. *Memories, Dreams, Reflections*, p. 306.

5. Cf. Friedrich Nötscher, *Altorientalischer und alttestamentlicher Auferstehungsglaube*, pp. 300ff. See also the literature cited there, as well as additional material by Josef Scharbert.

6. Cf. *ibid.*, p. 301.

7. Schopenhauer had already written that it is exactly here that the highly serious, important, celebrated and most dreadful character of the hour of death rests (*Parerga*, I, 245). This is a crisis in the strictest sense of the word—a Last Judgment.

8. *Zur Theologie des Todes*, p. 23, p.61.

9. Cf. G. Greshake and G. Lohfink, *Naherwartung, Auferstehung, Unsterblichkeit*, esp. pp. 170ff and p. 193. See also the works of Teilhard de Chardin.

10. C. G. Jung, *Psychology and Alchemy*, par. 26.

11. *Ego and Archetype*, p. 224.

12. As Aniela Jaffé does in *Apparitions and Precognition*.

13. *The Structure and Dynamics of the Psyche*, pars. 912, 923, 931, 948.

CHAPTER I

1. Cf., for example, K. Ranke, *Indogermanische Totenverehrung*, pp. 164ff. and the additional literature cited therein.

2. Cf. *ibid.*, p. 171.

3. *Ibid.*, p. 153.

4. *Ibid.*, p. 10, fns. 2, 3; see also p. 11.

5. Cf. François Cumont, *Lux Perpetua*, pp. 16f.

6. Cf. *ibid.*, p. 29.

7. Ranke, *op. cit.*, p. 153.

8. *Ibid.*, p. 176.

9. Cf. Ivan A. Lopatin, *The Cult of the Dead among the Natives of the Amur Basin*, esp. pp. 128f.

10. *Ibid.*, pp.126ff.

11. Cf. W. Kucher, *Jenseitsvorstellungen bei den verschiedenen Völkern*, p. 130.

12. Cf. Sigrid Lechner-Knecht, "Totenbräuche und Jenseitsvorstellungen bei den heutigen Indianern und bei asiatischen Völkern," pp. 165f.

13. *Corpus scriptorum latinorum academiae vindebonensis*, Vol. 47, 59.

14. Cf. G. R. S. Mead, *The Doctrine of the Subtle Body in Western Tradition*, pp. 82ff.

15. According to Greshake and Lohfink, this belief is rejected by most Catholic theologians today.

16. *Psychology and Religion*, pars. 553–555 (italics added).

17. Unfortunately, Origen's remarks on resurrection are preserved only in quotations in a Letter of St. Jerome to Pammachius, Book IV, 38. Cf. Mead, *op. cit.*, p. 83.

18. Mead, *op cit.*, p. 84.

19. *Ibid.*, p. 86.

20. Cf. *ibid.*, pp. 86f.

21. *Aegyptische Unterweltsbücher*, p. 136 (seventh hour of the night, seventh scene).

22. *Ibid.*, p. 333.

23. NN stands for the name of the deceased in question.

24. *Aegyptische Unterweltsbücher*, p. 336.

25. *Ibid.*, p. 339.

26. *Ibid.*, p. 348.

27. Cf. Jack Lindsay, *The Origins of Alchemy in Graeco-Roman Egypt*, p. 71.

28. *Ibid.*, p. 194.

29. *Ibid.*

30. *Ibid.*, p. 195.

31. *Ibid.*

32. *Ibid.* See also a saying of Hermes in Berthelot, *Collection des anciens alchemistes grecs:* "Go to the peasant Achaab and learn how he sows corn and harvests corn" (Vol. 2, p. 89).

33. Cited in G. Thausing (ed.), *Auferstehungsgedanke in ägyptischen religiösen Texten*, pp. 165f, Coffin text No. 58; Lacau, *Receuil des Traveaux*, 31.5.15; cf. also Coffin text 80, p. 166, fn.1.

34. *Das Totenbuch der Aegypter*, p. 215.

35. G. Thausing, *op. cit.*, p. 166.

36. From a Memphis Coffin text, cited by H. Kees, *Totenglauben und Jenseitsvorstellungen der alten Aegypter*, p. 148.

37. Pp. 306f.

38. According to H. Leisegang, *Die Gnosis*, pp. 68f.

39. *Ibid.*, pp. 69f.

40. In the "Egyptian Book of the Dead" he says: "I go down the river and up the river in the fields of bulrushes and I unite myself with the field of the sacrifice, for I am Ruti" (*Totenbuch der Aegypter*, p. 153).

41. Cf. Constant de Wit, *Le rôle et le sens du lion dans l'Egypte ancienne*, p. 161 and also p. 31. For the identity of Aker, see p. 129.

42. *Ibid.*, p. 169.

43. *Ibid.*, p. 141.

44. Cf. Kees, *op. cit.*, pp. 73ff.

45. Cf *Totenbuch der Aegypter*, p. 139.
46. Cf. de Wit, *op. cit.*, pp. 95, 97.
47. *Aegyptische Unterweltsbücher*, p. 443; see also p. 307.
48. *Ibid.*, p. 433.
49. *Ibid.*, p. 440.
50. *Ibid.*, p. 429; see also p. 347.
51. Cf. de Wit, *op. cit.*, p. 103.
52. An allusion to the washing of gold from river sand.
53. Cf. Berthelot, *op. cit.*, p. 71.
54. *Ibid.*, pp. 94f.
55. *Ibid.*, p. 95.
56. *Ibid.*
57. J.G. Griffiths, *Apuleius of Madura: The Isis Book*, p. 230 (italics added).
58. As quoted by the dreamer.
59. Shortly before this passage in the text, we read: "What sort of transformation do I observe now? How the water and fire, which originally had been inimical and antagonistic to each other and to their opposition, have now come together for the sake of unity and love" (p. 94, lines 17ff). Then follows the quoted passage concerning the "grave of Osiris."
60. Cf. Griffiths, *op. cit.*, p. 231. Griffiths' statement is based on A. A. Barb, "Diva Matrix," pp. 200f.
61. Edward Edinger, *Ego and Archetype*, pp. 209f.
62. *Ibid.*, p. 210.
63. *Psychodynamics of the Dying Process*, fig. 16b.
64. *Mysterium Mortis*, p. 85.
65. *Ibid.*, p. 89; see also p. 101.
66. *Ibid.*, p. 107.
67. Cf. *Aegyptische Unterweltsbücher*, p. 289; see also p. 273.
68. *Ibid.*, p. 290.

## CHAPTER 2

1. Among other things, the hero in *Green Mansions* adapts completely to the vegetation spirit of the Amazonian jungle.
2. *Ego and Archetype*, p. 212.
3. Cf. C. G. Jung, *Mysterium Coniunctionis*, par. 395.
4. *Adonis, Attis, Osiris.*
5. *Wald- und Feldkulte.*
6. *Ibid.*, Vol. 1, pp. 313ff.
7. *Ibid.*, pp. 410f.
8. Cf. V. Arnold-Döben, *Die Symbolik des Baumes im Manichaeismus*, Vol. 5, pp. 10ff.
9. *The Death of a Woman*, p. 269.
10. *Symbols of Transformation*, par. 367.
11. Reported in Kurt Lückel, *Begegnung mit Sterbenden*, p. 107.
12. The last sentence of the dream is not clearly formulated, for the dying

man could no longer speak coherently. What he meant was that red drops formed a kind of staircase and, as he ascended it, he saw a Christmas tree above him. This, at any rate, is how the wife of the deceased interpreted this passage in the dream to me.

13. In *Alchemical Studies*, pars. 304–482.

14. Iman 'Abd ar-Rahim ibn Ahmad al-Qadi, *Das Totenbuch des Islam*, p. 179.

15. *The Archetypes and the Collective Unconscious*, par. 198 (italics added).

16. Berthelot, *Collection des anciens alchimistes grecs*, Vol. 2, p. 290. The name "Komarios" probably came from the Aramaic *komar*, meaning "priest."

17. *Ibid.*, p. 292.

18. Cf. Zosimos, in Berthelot, *op. cit.*, p. 107. The uniform, single nature is attributed to the hard surface of the metals and the flexible wooden nature of the plants.

19. Olympiodorus, in Berthelot, *op. cit.*, p. 94. There are two whitenings and two yellowings, and two combined substances, wet and dry. This means that in the catalog for "Yellow," for example, we read: "Plants and metals. . . . Yellow plants are the crocus and the elydrion," etc. Or: "Plants are all yellowish-gold ores (= stones)" (*Ibid.*, p. 6).

20. Berthelot, *op. cit.*, p. 292.

21. *Ibid.*, p. 293.

22. Jorinde Ebert, "Parinirvana," p. 299.

23. *Memories, Dreams, Reflections*, p. 314.

24. In *Spiritual Body and Celestial Earth*, Chapter I, 3, "Visionary Geography," pp. 24–36.

25. *Ibid.*, pp. 30f.

26. *Ibid.*, pp. 31–32.

27. *Ibid.*, p. 32.

28. Cf. N. Junker, *Die Stundenwachen in den Osirismysterien*, Vol. 4, pp. 2, 4; see also A. Moret, *Mystères Egyptiens*, pp. 22ff.

29. Cf. Moret, *op. cit.*, p. 33.

30. *Totenbuch der Aegypter*, p. 167.

31. *Ibid.*, p. 149.

32. *Ibid.*, p. 170.

33. Cf. Mokusen Miyuki, *Kreisen des Lichtes*, p. 176.

34. *Ibid.* Cf. also C. G. Jung and Richard Wilhelm, *The Secret of the Golden Flower*.

35. cf. Miyuki, *op. cit.*, p. 69.

36. *Ibid.*

37. *Ibid.*, p. 80.

38. *Ibid.*, p. 92.

39. *Ibid.*, p. 111.

40. Cf. Sigrid Lochner-Knecht, *Totenbräuche und Jenseitsvorstellungen bei den heutigen Indianern*, pp. 169–170.

41. *Ibid.*, p. 163.

42. In *Die Märchen der Weltliteratur: Zigeuner Märchen*. Many variations of this fairy tale are to be found in Eastern Europe.

43. For details, see M.-L. von Franz, *Die Visionen des Niklaus von Flüe.*

44. Cf. the roses and other flowers painted by David Eldred's patient, in *Psychodynamics of the Dying Process*, esp. figs. 12, 15, 26, 27.

45. Cf. Paul Arnold, *Das Totenbuch der Maya.* Cf. also A. Anderson and Charles Dibble, *Florentine Codex*, Book 3, *passim.*

46. Arnold, *op. cit.*, p. 18.

47. *Ibid.*, pp. 38, 39.

48. *Ibid.*, pp. 43, 185.

49. *Ibid.*, pp. 57, 95ff.

50. Marcel Granet, *La Pensée Chinoise: Chinese Thought*, p. 267.

51. *Ibid.*

52. *Ibid.*, p. 160.

53. Granet, *Danses et Légendes de la Chine ancienne*, pp. 332, 335; see also p. 333.

54. *Ibid.*, p. 159.

55. *Ibid.*, p. 334, p. 330 and fn.

56. *Ibid.*, p. 158.

57. Cf. J. Wiesner, *Grab und Jenseits*, p. 218.

58. This miraculous flower appeared as a motif for the first time in one of the analysand's previous dreams; this is why she refers to it in the active imagination.

CHAPTER 3

1. Presumably with the *hydor theion*, that is, with the "divine water."

2. In the text it reads, "from the smoke," which does not fit the context well. Smoke, for the alchemists, was a symbol for sublimated material.

3. Berthelot, *Collection*, Vol. 2, pp. 293ff, pars. 10ff.

4. "Pardes Rimmonim" is the title of an old Cabbalistic tract by Moses Cordovero (sixteenth century). "In Cabbalistic doctrine Malchuth and Tifereth . . . represent the female and male principles within the Godhead." Note by Aniela Jaffé in *Memories, Dreams, Reflections*, p. 294.

5. *Memories*, pp. 293–295.

6. *Letters*, Vol. 1, pp. 358f.

7. Cf. Sixtus of Siena, *Biblioteca SanctaVenetiis*, p. 478. See also Martin Grabmann, *Die echten Schriften des hl. Thomas von Aquin*, p. 189. Further in M.-L. von Franz, *Aurora Consurgens, passim.*

8. von Franz, *Aurora Consurgens*, p. 145.

9. *Ibid.*, pp. 145, 147.

10. *Ego and Archetype*, p. 217.

11. Cf. von Franz, *Number and Time*, p. 172.

12. Cf. von Franz,"Some Archetypes surrounding Death," p. 14.

13. This body, however, as is evident in the dream, is no longer the "old" body, but a new spiritualized one.

14. *The Death of a Woman*, p. 28.

15. Cited in *Leben und Tod in den Religionen*, p. 178.

16. *Ibid.*, p. 203.
17. In *Zigeuner Märchen*, pp. 117ff.
18. In *Französische Märchen*, p. 141. See also *Bretonische Märchen*, pp. 1ff.
19. Cf. M.-L. von Franz, *The Passion of Perpetua*, pp. 11, 13.
20. This statement is based entirely on the profound and subtle expositions of Henri Corbin in *Spiritual Body and Celestial Earth*, esp. pp. 3–105.
21. *Ibid.*, p. 15; see also p. 38.
22. *Ibid.*, pp. 28, 36, 42.
23. *Ibid.*, p. 42.
24. *Ibid.*
25. *Ibid.*
26. M.-L. von Franz, "Some Archetypes surrounding Death," p. 13.
27. Barbara Hannah, "Regression oder Erneuerung im Alter," p. 191.
28. *Ibid.*, pp. 191ff.
29. *Traumbuch*, p. 207.
30. Cf. Emily Vermeule, *Aspects of Death in Early Greek Art and Poetry*. The illustrations in this volume are very meaningful but the text is often superficial.
31. Cited, Mircea Eliade, *Von Zalmoxis zu Dschingis-Khan*, p. 239. As Eliade points out, this beautiful poem is almost impossible to translate. A rough translation of Eliade's French version reads as follows: "Tell them that I have freed / an unsurpassable queen / promised from the universe; / that in this wedding / a star spun the thread, / that sun and moon / held the crown / over the throne; / the mountains were my priests, / beechtrees my witnesses; / that the hymns were the songs / of the forest birds; / that I had the virgin stars / as candles, / thousands of birds / and bright constellations."
32. Cited, Edgar Herzog, *Psyche and Death*, p. 107.
33. *Ibid.* Cf. also the other beautiful material cited therein, including Bürger's "Leonore" and its English parallels in John Radford, "An Image of Death in Dreams and Ballads," pp. 15ff.
34. Günther Roeder, *Urkunden zur Religion des alten Aegypten*, p. 37 (fifth hour).
35. *Ibid.*, p. 38.
36. *Ibid.*
37. *Ibid.* Cf. also pp. 195f, where the deceased is addressed as Osiris: "Your sister Isis comes to you, joyful out of love for you. You place her upon your phallus and your semen streams into her."
38. Cf. Joseph Wiesner, *Grab und Jenseits*, pp. 175ff.

## CHAPTER 4

1. The *I Ching*, Vol. 1, p. 250.
2. *Totenbuch der Aegypter*, p. 348.
3. *Ibid.*, p. 174.
4. *Ibid.*, Rubric 42, p. 115. Cf. also *Aegyptische Unterweltsbücher*, p. 371.
5. *Aegyptische Unterweltsbücher*, p. 325; see also p. 298.
6. *Life after Life* and *Reflections on Life after Life*.

7. *Recollections of Death.*

8. *Sterben ist doch ganz anders.*

9. See also J. Lindley, "Near Death Experiences."

10. Johann Christoph Hampe, *op. cit.*, pp. 52–57.

11. *Ibid.*, p. 83.

12. *Ibid.*, p. 89.

13. *Psychodynamics of the Dying Process.* p. 181.

14. Cf. also Lindley, *op. cit.*, p. 110: "I was inside a black river. Everything was darkness. I was alone and suffering terribly and waves were washing me to and fro. A voice spoke behind me: 'This is the River of Death. . . . This is eternity. You're lost. This is eternity.' " See also p. 114: a genuine vision of hell.

15. Cf. Emily Vermeule, *Aspects of Death*, pp. 37–41.

16. *And a Time to Die, p. 107.*

17. Rahim, *Das Totenbuch des Islam*, pp. 141f.

18. *Ibid.*, pp. 51ff.

19. In the final analysis, this is a variant of the primal image of the nocturnal sea journey. In this connection, cf. Uwe Steffen, *Das Mysterium von Tod und Auferstehung.*

20. Helmut Brunner, "Unterweltsbücher in ägyptischen Königsgräben," pp. 224f. Soker is an old god of death.

21. Cf. Theo Grundermaier, "Todesriten und Lebenssymbole in den afrikanischen Religionen," pp. 250ff.

22. Cf. Detlef I. Lauf, "Im Zeichen des grossen Uebergangs," p. 95.

23. Berthelot, *Collection*, Vol. 2, p. 296, Sec. 4.

24. Cf. R. Moody, *Life after Life*, pp. 30–34.

25. Esp. *On Death and Dying.* Chapter 5, *passim.*

26. "Jenseits des Todes," pp. 74f.

27. *Reflections on Life after Life*, pp. 18ff.

28. *Ibid.*, p. 19.

29. Cited Fortier, *Dreams and Preparation for Death*, p. 1. This excellent study reports the dream series of three dying patients.

30. *Ibid.*

31. See D. I. Lauf, *op. cit.*, pp. 42ff.

32. Christa Meves, *op. cit.*, p. 75.

33. Edward Whitmont, *The Symbolic Quest*, p. 53.

34. Plural of *ba*. According to the view of the Egyptians, the immortal volatile part of the soul.

35. Helmut Brunner, *op. cit.*, p. 221.

36. *Ibid.*, p. 228.

37. *Memories, Dreams, Reflections*, p. 269.

38. Cf. F. Cumont, *Lux Perpetua*, pp. 49ff. Light also drives away demons; I thank René Malamud for calling this to my attention.

## CHAPTER 5

1. "Ich habe Angst zu sterben," pp. 73f. Lindner cites this dream from J. E. Meyer, *Tod und Neurose*, pp. 18f.

2. *Ego and Archetype*, p. 200.

3. *Begegnung mit Sterbenden*, pp. 95f.

4. *Psyche and Death*, p. 39.

5. *Ibid.*, p. 43.

6. *Ibid.*, p. 44.

7. *Memories, Dreams, Reflections*, p. 313.

8. *Ibid.*, pp. 313–14.

9. Examples in Herzog, *op. cit.*, p. 51.

10. *Ibid.*, p. 53.

11. "Sterbeerfahrungen psychologisch beleuchtet."

12. *Ibid.*, p. 33.

13. One is reminded of the novel of the same title by Jeremias Gotthelf.

14. Berthelot, *La chimie du Moyen Age*, Vol. 3. p. 117; cited, Jung, *Alchemical Studies*, par. 424.

15. Jung, *op. cit.*, par. 428.

16. Hoghelande, "De alchemiae difficultatibus," p. 160; cited, Jung, *op. cit.*, par. 429.

17. Cf. Osis and Haraldson, *At the Hour of Death*, pp. 51, 54, 209ff.

18. *Ibid.*, pp. 105, 112.

19. This experience of the attractive "other" is described by Thomas Mann in *Death in Venice*; there, of course, the "other" does not appear as an inner figure but is projected onto an outer individual.

20. Cf. K. Kerenyi, *Hermes der Seelenführer*, p. 94.

21. Cf. the impressive presentation of the fetching of the Prince by a beautiful "unknown woman" in Giuseppe di Lampedusa's novel, *The Leopard*.

22. *Spiritual Body and Celestial Earth*, pp. 42ff.

23. *Ibid.*, p. 42.

24. Cf. G. Widengren, *Mani und der Manichaeismus*, p. 33.

25. *Coptic Khephalaia*, Chapter 114; cited Widengren, op. cit., p. 66.

26. *Ibid.*, p. 106.

27. Henri Corbin, *Creative Imagination in the Sufism of Ibn 'Arabi*, p. 279.

28. Cf. W. Neumann, *Der Mensch und sein Doppelgänger*, p. 157.

29. Corbin, *op. cit.*, pp. 384f.

30. *Ibid.*, pp. 388f.

31. *Life after Life*, pp. 62f.

32. *Ibid.*, p. 102.

33. Hampe, *Sterben ist doch ganz anders*, p. 89; from the account of the patient as reported by Dr. Werner Duvernoy of Uppsala.

34. A. Jaffé, *Apparitions and Precognition*, p. 20.

35. *Ibid.*, pp. 45f; cf. also pp. 105ff.

## CHAPTER 6

1. P.1.
2. Berthelot, *Collection*, Vol. 2, pp. 151f.
3. *Ibid.*, p. 201.
4. *Ibid.*, p. 211. Literally, "according to the philosophers."
5. *Ibid.*, p. 252.
6. *Sterben ist doch ganz anders*, p. 71; cited, A. Sborowitz, *Der leidende Mensch*, p. 56.
7. Cf. Jacques le Goff, *The Birth of Purgatory*. My thanks to Prof. Luigi Aurigemma for calling this volume to my attention.
8. *Ibid.*, pp. 49f.
9. *Ibid.*, p. 55.
10. *Ibid.*, p. 61.
11. *Ibid.*, pp. 67ff.
12. Cf. *ibid.*, pp. 74f.
13. Cf. *ibid.*, pp. 29ff.
14. Cf. *ibid.*, pp. 82ff.
15. *Ibid.*, pp. 92ff.
16. As documented, *ibid.*, pp. 81f.
17. Stromata, iv, 24; vii, 6. Cf. also Origen, in *Exodum homiliae* 6, *Patrologia graeca*, xiii, 334–5.
18. Cf. *Aegyptischer Unterweltsbücher*, p. 249.
19. *Ibid.*, p. 211.
20. Cf. *ibid.*, p. 181.
21. Cf. Jung, *The Structure and Dynamics of the Psyche*, par. 26.
22. *Ibid.*, pars. 114ff.
23. Fragment 30; in Freeman, *Ancilla to the Pre-Socratic Philosophers*, p. 26.
24. Cf. Jung, *Psychology and Alchemy*, pars. 404, 473.
25. *Das physikalische Weltbild der Antike*, pp. 219ff.
26. In *Structure and Dynamics*, pars. 441–42.
27. *Ibid.*, par. 441 (italics added).
28. Pp. 3ff.
29. *Ibid.*, p. 39.
30. *Ibid.*, p. 125.
31. In Plutarch, *De genio Socratis*, chpts. 21ff.
32. M. Ninck, *Die Bedeutung des Wassers im Kult und Leben der Alten*, pp. 115f.
33. Cf. Jung, *Alchemical Studies*, par. 101.
34. Cf. G. Roeder, *Urkunden zur Religion des alten Aegypten*, p. 195.
35. *Ibid.*
36. *Totenbuch der Aegypter*, pp. 313ff.
37. G. Thausing, "Altägyptisches religiöses Gedankengut im heutigen Afrika," p. 142; see also p. 92 and p. 133.
38. Cf. Robert Steuer, *Ueber das wohlriechende Natron bei den alten Aegyptern*, pp. 23f.

39. Roeder, *op. cit.*, p. 302.

40. A. Moret, *Mystères Egyptiens*, p. 27.

41. Cf. D. I. Lauf, "Nachtodzustand und Wiedergeburt in den Traditionen der tibetanischen Totenbuchs," p. 95.

42. Cited, Hampe, *op. cit.*, p. 83.

43. *Ibid.*, p. 85.

44. *Ibid.*, p. 91.

45. Jung, *Letters*, Vol. 2, p. 146, fn. 1.

46. *Ibid.*, p. 146.

47. Jung, *Mysterium Coniunctionis*, par. 691.

48. *Ibid.*, par. 704.

49. Hampe, *op. cit.*, p. 93.

50. Cf. also, for example, Michael Sabom, *Recollections of Death*, pp. 45ff, 51ff.

## Chapter 7

1. Barbara Hannah, "Regression oder Erneuerung im Alten," p. 198.

2. *Ibid.*, pp. 199ff.

3. *Ibid.*, p. 200.

4. Cf. Jung, *Psychology and Religion*, pars. 387–402, esp. par. 400.

5. Cited, Hampe, *Sterben ist doch ganz anders*, p. 96. (italics added).

6. Cf. G. Roeder, *Urkunden zur Religion*, p. 297.

7. *Ibid.*, pp. 297ff.

8. "The dreamer had browsed in Ginsberg's *Legends of the Jews* at the home of a friend" (Edinger, *Ego and Archetype*, p. 215).

9. That unknown other! (author's note).

10. *Ego and Archetype*, pp. 214f.

11. *Mysterium Coniunctionis*, par. 778.

12. *And a Time to Die*, p. 109 (italics added).

13. *Letters*, Vol. 2, p. 146, fn. 1.

14. *Ibid.*, pp. 145f.

15. Cf. Rolf Hofmann, *Die wichtigsten Körpersgottheiten im Huang t'ung ching*, p. 25, pp. 27ff. The text of the *Huang t'ung ching* refers to ideas from the earlier Han period.

16. Cf. *ibid.*, p. 26.

17. For taoistic alchemy, cf. Lu K'uan Yü, *Taoist Yoga*.

18. Hofmann, *op. cit.*, p. 29; see also pp. 39, 45.

19. Cf Ajit Mookerjee, *Tantra Asana*, p. 5.

20. *Ibid.*, p. 42.

21. *Ibid.*, p. 195.

22. Cf. J. F. Sproktoff, "Der feindliche Tote," p. 271.

23. Arnold Mindell, in his *Dreambody*, has made a beginning.

24. Cf. Jung, *The Spirit in Man, Art, and Literature*, par. 22.

25. *Ibid.*, par. 29 (from the *Labyrinthus medicorum*, Chapter 2).

26. *Ibid.*, pars. 39f, and Jung, *Alchemical Studies*, par. 168.

27. Cf. *ibid.*, par. 171.
28. Cited, Hampe, *op. cit.*, pp. 102f.
29. *Ibid.*, p. 109.
30. *Ibid.*, pp. 73f.
31. Jung, *op. cit.*, pars. 85–87.
32. *Ibid.*, par. 86.
33. *Ibid.*
34. *Ibid* (Greek terms added).
35. *Ibid.*, par. 87.
36. From a treatise called "Apokalypsis Heremetis," ascribed by Huser to Paracelsus; in *Epistolarum medicinalium Conradi Gessneri*, Book I, fol. 2r; cited, Jung, *op. cit.*, par. 166.
37. Cf. Jung, *op. cit.*, par. 86, fn. 4.
38. *Mystères Egyptiens*, p. 75.
39. That is, to "die of your sorrow" or "cling to *(dmj ḥr)* life" (H. Jacobsohn, "The Dialogue of a World-Weary Man with His Ba," p. 45).
40. *Ibid.*, p. 44. See also Barbara Hannah, *Encounters with the Soul*, p. 103, for an alternate translation.
41. H. Jacobsohn, *op. cit.*, p. 47.
42. Hampe, *op. cit.*, p. 74.

CHAPTER 8

1. *Life after Life*, p. 102.
2. *Ibid.*, p. 104.
3. Hampe, *Sterben ist doch ganz anders*, pp. 92f.
4. *Memories, Dreams, Reflections*, pp. 290f.
5. Cf. G. A. Gaskell, *Dictionary of All Scriptures and Myths*, p. 93; cited, Fortier, *Dreams and Preparation for Death*, p. 157.
6. "Sterbeerfahrungen psychologisch beleuchtet," p. 34.
7. *Ibid.*
8. *Ego and Archetype*, p. 218.
9. Moody, *op. cit.*, p. 49.
10. Cf. Jung, *Mysterium Coniunctionis*, par. 129.
11. *Ibid.*, par. 133.
12. Cf. also in this connection Jung, *Memories*, pp. 321f.
13. See above, Introduction.
14. *Letters*, Vol. 1, pp. 256–58.
15. Hence the silliness of most spiritistic communications with ghosts (author's note).
16. Jung, *op. cit.*, pars. 257–58.
17. Moody, *op. cit.*, p. 54.
18. *Ibid.*
19. *Memories*, pp. 296f.
20. Cf. J. Haekel, "Religion," p. 45.
21. Cf. W. Kucher, *Jenseitsvorstellungen bei den verschiedenen Völkern*, p. 90.

22. *Ibid.*, p. 11.
23. I. Paulson, "Seelenvorstellungen und Totenglaube bei nordischen Völkern," pp. 84ff.
24. *Pretiosa margarita novella*, p. 121.
25. For this and the following, cf. Richard Wilhelm, *Weisheit des Ostens*, pp. 25ff.
26. Italics added.
27. Jung, *Letters*, Vol. 1, pp. 436f.
28. Jung is referring here to the consciousness of the Self.
29. Jung, *op. cit.*, p. 437.
30. The patient described by Eldred in *The Psychodynamics of the Dying Process* seems to have been such a case.
31. Cf. also Jung, *Letters*, Vol. 1: "It is just as if the soul detached itself from the body sometimes years before death actually occurs, or sometimes with perfectly healthy people who are going to die within a short delay by acute illness or accident. As far as we know at all there seems to be no immediate decomposition of the soul" (p. 438).
32. *Ibid.*, p. 436.
33. Wilhelm, *op. cit.*, p. 26.
34. *Ibid.*, p. 30.
35. Cf. Mokusen Miyuki, *Kreisen des Lichts*, p. 200.
36. *Ibid.*, p. 201, fn. 88.
37. *Ibid.*, p. 204, fn. 86 (also written as "millet seed").

## CHAPTER 9

1. According to the Paris Codex of 1478.
2. *"ho chous"*—literally, "rubble," here the earthly-concrete.
3. Berthelot, *Collection*, Vol. 2, pp. 296ff, pars. 15–16.
4. *Ibid.*, pp. 298f.
5. P. 39: cited, Jung, *Psychology and Alchemy*, par. 374.
6. *Aegyptische Unterweltsbücher*, p. 38.
7. *Ibid.*, p. 37.
8. H. Jacobsohn, "Das göttliche Wort und der göttliche Stein," p. 231.
9. Cf. G. Thausing, *Altägyptisches religiöses Gedankengut im heutigen Afrika*, p. 91.
10. For the following, cf. Bernard Uhde, "Psyche ein Symbol?" pp. 103ff.
11. *Ibid.*, p. 110.
12. *The Histories*, II, 123.
13. *Aegyptische Unterweltsbücher*, pp. 204, 263, 330–333.
14. Cf. H. Corbin, *Spiritual Body and Celestial Earth*, pp. 37f.
15. "The island of Prokonessos was the site of the famous Greek marble quarry, now called Marmara (Turkey)" (Jung, *Alchemical Studies*, par. 87, fn. 14).
16. *Ibid.*, par. 87.
17. *Ibid.*, par. 86.

18. *Ibid.*, pars. 91ff.
19. Cf. *ibid.*, par. 118.
20. *Ibid.*, par. 112.
21. Cf. *ibid.*, pars. 118–19.
22. Cf. H. Jacobsohn, *op. cit.*, pp. 234f.
23. *Memories, Dreams, Reflections*, p. 290.
24. *Ibid.*, p.291.
25. von Franz, *C. G. Jung: His Myth in Our Time*, p. 287.
26. *Memories*, p. 4.
27. *Alchemical Studies*, par. 120.
28. Cf. Roeder, *Urkunden*, p. 298.
29. *Sterben ist doch ganz anders*, p. 71.
30. Cf. F. Cumont, *Lux Perpetua*, p. 24 and illustration.
31. Cited, J. Ebert, "Parinirvana," p. 287, p. 289.
32. Barbara Hannah, *Jung: His Life and Work*, p. 344.
33. *Ibid.*
34. *Ibid.*
35. *Memories*, p. 225.
36. *Ego and Archetype*, pp. 220–21.
37. *Alchemical Studies*, par. 119.
38. *Ibid.*, par. 127.
39. *Ibid.*
40. *Ibid.*
41. P. 211.
42. David Eldred, *Psychodynamics of the Dying Process*, p. 171.

CHAPTER 10

1. Cf. E. Mattiesen, *Das persönliche Ueberleben des Todes, passim*.
2. *Letters*, Vol, 2, p. 44.
3. In the *Commentary on the Golden Verses*; see G. R. S. Mead, *The Doctrine of the Subtle Body in Western Tradition*, pp. 63f.
4. *Lexikon der Suidas*, p. 194.
5. Par. 414. Cited, Mead, *op. cit.*, pp. 59f.
6. Mead's "spiritous body" or "spirit-body," *op. cit.*, pp. 33ff.
7. *De sera numinis vindicta*, xxii, p. 564.
8. Mead, *op.cit.*, pp. 42f.
9. *Sententiae ad intelligibilia descendentes*, xxix, pp. 13f; cited, Mead, *op. cit.*, p. 45.
10. *Philoponi in Aristotelis de Anima*, 9, 35f; 10, 42f; cited Mead, *op. cit.*, pp. 48f.
11. Mead, p. 51.
12. Cf. Jung, *Alchemical Studies*, pars. 85–144.
13. *Spiritual Body*, pp. 180–221.
14. *Ibid.*, pp. 90ff.
15. Moody's "being of light," *Life after Life*, pp. 58ff.

16. In *Sententiae ad intelligibilia descendentes*, Porphyry's summary of Plotinian doctrine, pp. 14f. Cf. Mead, *op. cit.*, pp. 61ff.

17. *Commentaries on the Timeaus of Plato*, 384 AB, 848.

18. Cf. Mead, p. 63.

19. Cited, Jaffé, *Apparitions and Precognition*, p. 66.

20. *Ibid.*

21. According to Sheikh Ahmad, only the quintessence of this aspect of the collective unconscious survives the death of the individual and remains preserved, so to speak, in its "spirit body."

22. *Letters*, Vol. 1, p. 257 (italics added).

23. *Ibid.*, p. 256.

24. *Memories*, p. 325.

25. Cf. von Franz, *Projection and Re-Collection in Jungian Psychology*, pp. 95ff.

26. *Letters*, Vol. 1, p. 343.

## CHAPTER 11

1. Sir John Eccles, the celebrated brain specialist, has recently postulated the independence of one part of the psyche from the brain. See *The Human Brain*; also Wilder Penfield, *The Mystery of the Mind*.

2. *Letters*, Vol. 2, p. 45.

3. *The Tao of Physics*, p. 188.

4. *Letters*, Vol. 1, p. 433.

5. *Dreams: God's Forgotten Language*, p. 60.

6. *Mysterium Coniunctionis*, par. 763.

7. Cf. von Franz, *Aurora Consurgens*, p. 379.

8. *Sterben ist doch ganz anders*, p. 126.

9. *Ibid.*, pp. 81f ( italics added).

10. "Near Death Experiences," p. 111.

11. Cf. A. Jaffé, *Apparitions*, pp. 175f.

12. Cf. Jung, *Psychology and Alchemy*, pars. 201–208.

13. Telepathy, for example (author's note).

14. *Letters*, Vol. 1, pp. 117f.

15. *Letters*, Vol. 2, p. 561.

16. *Op. cit.*, p. 182 (italics added).

17. *Op. cit.*, p. 51.

18. *Ibid.*, p. 58.

19. *Ibid.*

20. *Ibid.*, p. 59.

21. *Das persönliche Ueberleben des Todes*, Vol. 1, p. 90.

22. Cf. also the light appearances, *ibid.*, p. 93, 112; Vol. 2, p. 261; Vol. 2, p. 313, where such a light appears during an out-of-the-body experience.

23. Cited, Mattiesen, *op. cit.*, Vol. 3, p. 25.

24. *Ibid.*, p. 171.

25. *Ibid.*, p.189.

26. Cf. F. Capra, *op. cit.*, p. 211.

27. *Wholeness and the Implicate Order.*
28. *Ibid.*, p. 71.
29. Cf. *ibid.*, p. 72.
30. Bohm, *op. cit.*, pp. 147ff.
31. *Ibid.*, p. 151.
32. *Ibid.*, p. 186.
33. *Ibid.*, p. 209.
34. Cf. also S. Grof, *Die Erfahrung des Todes*, pp. 157ff.
35. Bohm, *op. cit.*, esp. p. 210.
36. *Op. cit.*, esp. pp. 230ff.
37. *Précis of Special Relativity*, p. 14.
38. *L'Esprit cet Inconnu.*
39. Cf. also W. Cazenave, *La Science et l'âme du Monde.*
41. Cf. Hubert Reeves, *Patience dans l'Azur*, pp. 245f.
40. Cf. also M. Sabom, *Recollections of Death*, pp. 51ff.
42. Cf. A. Vorbichler, "Das Leben im Rhythmus von Tod und Wiedergeburt in der Vorstellung der schwarzafrikanischen Völker": "In this religious . . . tradition there is also death and everything that belongs to it. Death is in no way an end but only a transition into another state of being within the community" (p. 230).
43. Theo Sundermeier, "Todesriten und Lebenssymbole in den afrikanischen Religionen," p. 256.
44. *Letters*, Vol. 1, p. 569.

# Bibliography

*Aegyptische Unterweltsbücher.* Edited by Erik Hornung. Zurich/Munich: Artemis, 1972.

Aichele, W. (ed.). *Die Märchen der Weltliteratur:*
—*Französische Märchen.* Jena: Diederichs, 1923.
—*Zigeuner Märchen.* Jena: Diederichs, 1926.
—*Bretonische Märchen.* Dusseldorf/Cologne: Diederichs, 1959.

Aichlin, H.; Feist, D.; Herzog, R.; Lindner, R; Pohlhammer, H. G. *Tod un Sterben.* Gütersloh/Munich: Siebenstern, 1978.

Anders, Ferdinand. *Das Pantheon der Maya.* Graz: Akademische Druck- und Verlagsanstalt, 1963.

Anderson, A.; Dibble, Charles Elliott (eds.). *The Florentine Codex.* Santa Fe, 1978.

Arnold, Paul. *Das Totenbuch der Maya.* Bern/Munich/Vienna: Scherz, 1980.

Arnold-Döbin, V. "Die Symbolik des Baumes im Manichaeismus," *Symbolon,* Vol. 5. Cologne: Brill, 1980.

Artemidorus of Daldes. *Traumbuch.* Translated by F. Kraus. Basel/Stuttgart: Schwabe, 1965. English version: *Judgement or Exposition of Dreams.* London: 1606.

Barb, A. A. "Diva Matrix," *Journal of the Warburg and Courtauld Institute,* No. 16, pp. 200ff. London, 1963.

Berthelot, M. *La chimie au Moyen Age.* 3 volumes. Reproduction of the 1893 edition. Osnabrück: Otto Zeller, 1967.

————. *Collection des anciens alchimistes grecs.* 3 volumes. Reproduction of the 1888 (Paris) edition. Osnabrück: Otto Zeller, 1967.

Bohm, David. *Wholeness and the Implicate Order.* London/Boston/Henley: Routledge & Kegan Paul, 1980.

Bonus, Petrus. *Pretiosa margarita novella.* Edited by Joannes Lacinius. Venice, 1546.

Boros, Ladislaus. *The Mystery of Death.* New York: Crossroad, 1973.

Bozzano, E. *Uebersinnliche Erscheinungen bei Naturvölkern.* Bern: Francke, 1948.

*Bretonische Märchen.* See Aichele, W.

Brunner, Helmut. "Unterweltsbücher in ägyptischen Königsgräben." In: *Leben und Tod in den Religionen.*

Capra, Fritjof. *The Tao of Physics.* Boulder (Colo.): Shambala, 1976.

Cazenave, M. *La Science et l'Ame du Monde.* Paris: Imago, 1983.

Charon, J. *L'Esprit cet Inconnu.* Paris: Albin Michel, 1977.

Clarus, Ingeborg. *Du stirbst, damit du lebst: Aegyptische Mythologie in tiefenpsychologischer Sicht.* Fellbach: Bonz, 1980.

Clement of Alexandria. *Stromata.* In: *The Writings of Clement of Alexandria.* Translated by William Wilson. (Ante-Nicene Christian Library, 4, 12.) Edinburgh: 1867, 2 vols.

Corbin, Henri. *Creative Imagination in the Sufism of Ibn 'Arabi.* Translated by Ralph Manheim. (Bollingen Series XCI.) Princeton: Princeton University Press, 1969.

———. *Spiritual Body and Celestial Earth: From Mazdean Iran to Shi'ite Iran*. Translated by Nancy Pearson. (Bollingen Series XCI:2.) Princeton: Princeton University Press, 1977.

Costa de Beauregard, Olivier. *Précis of Special Relativity*. Translated by B. Hoffman. Academy Press, 1966.

Cumont, François. *Lux perpetua*. Paris: Genthner, 1949.

Damascius. *Commentaries on Plato's Parmenides*. Paris: 1889.

Dibble, Charles Elliott. See Anderson, A.

Ebert, Jorinde. "Parinirvana." In: *Leben und Tod in den Religionen*.

Eccles, John. *The Human Psyche*. Berlin/New York: Springer, 1980.

Edinger Edward. *Ego and Archetype: Individuation and the Religious Function of the Psyche*. New York: Putnam's Sons, for the C. G. Jung Foundation, 1972.

Eldred, David. *The Psychodynamics of the Dying Process: An Analysis of the Dreams and Paintings of a Terminally Ill Woman*. Dissertation, University of Michigan, 1982. Unpublished.

Eliade, Mircea. *Von Zalmoxis zu Dschingis-Kahn: Religion und Volkskultur in Süd-Ost-Europa*. Cologne: Hohenheim, 1982.

Espagnat, B. *A la Recherche du Réel*. Paris: Gauthier, 1980.

Feist, D. See Aichlin, H.

Fortier, Millie Kelly. *Dreams and Preparation for Death*. Dissertation. Ann Arbor/London: University Microfilms International, 1972.

Franz, Marie-Louise von. "Archetypes Surrounding Death," *Quadrant*, Vol. 12, No. 1 (Summer 1979).

———. *Aurora Consurgens: A Document Attributed to Thomas Aquinas on the Problem of Opposites in Alchemy*. Translated by R. F. C. Hull and A. S. B. Glover. New York: Pantheon Books, 1966.

———. *C. G. Jung: His Myth in Our Time*. Translated by William H. Kennedy. New York: Putnam's Sons for C. G. Jung Foundation, 1975.

———. *Number and Time: Reflections Leading toward a Unification of Depth Psychology and Physics*. Translated by Andrea Dykes. Evanston (Ill.): Northwestern University Press, 1974.

———. *The Passion of Perpetua*. Irving (Texas): Spring Publications, 1979.

———. *Projection and Re-Collection in Jungian Psychology: Reflections of the Soul*. Translated by William H. Kennedy. La Salle (Ill.)/London: Open Court, 1980.

———. *Die Visionen des Niklaus von Flüe*. Zurich: Daimon, 1980.

———; Frey-Rohn, Liliane; Jaffé, Aniela. *Im Umkreis des Todes*. Zurich: Daimon, 1980.

*Französische Märchen*. See Aichele, W.

Frazer, J. G. *Adonis, Attis, Osiris*. London: Macmillan, 1906.

Freeman, Kathleen. *Ancilla to the Pre-Socratic Philosophers*. Cambridge: Harvard University Press, 1957.

Frey-Rohn, Liliane. "Sterbeerfahrungen psychologisch beleuchtet." In: Franz, Marie-Louise von, et al., *Im Umkreis des Todes, pp. 29–95*.

Gaskell, G. A. *A Dictionary of All Scriptures and Myths*. New York: Julian Press, 1960.

Gotthelf, Jeremias. *Die schwarze Spinne*. Bern: Stämpfli, 1979.

Grabmann, Martin. *Die echten Schriften des hl. Thomas von Aquin*. Münster: 1920.

Granet, Marcel. *Danses et Légendes de la Chine Ancienne*. Paris: Presses Universitaires de France, 1959.

————. *La Pensée Chinoise: Chinese Thought*. Ayer Company, 1975.

Greshake, Gisbert; Lohfink, Gerhard. *Naherwartung, Auferstehung, Unsterblichkeit*. Freiburg/Basel/Vienna: Herder, 1978.

Griffiths, J. G. *Apuleius of Madura: The Isis Book*. Leiden:Brill, 1975.

Grof, Stanislav. "Die Erfahrung des Todes," *Integrative Therapie*, 2, 3 (1980).

Grof, Stanislav; Halifax, Joan. *The Human Encounter with Death*. New York: Dutton, 1978.

Grundermeier, Theo. "Todesriten und Lebenssymbole in den afrikanischen Religionen." In: *Leben und Tod in den Religionen*.

Haekel, J. "Religion." In: *Lehrbuch der Völkerkunde*.

Hampe, Johann Christoph. *Sterben ist doch ganz anders: Erfahrungen mit dem eigenen Tod*. Berlin: Kreuz Verlag, 1975.

Hannah, Barbara. *Encounters with the Soul: Active Imagination as Developed by C. G. Jung*. Santa Monica: Sigo Press, 1981.

————. *Jung: His Life and Work: A Biographical Memoir*. New York; Putnam's Sons, 1976.

————. "Regression oder Erneuerung im Alter." In: *Psychotherapeutische Probleme*, pp. 175–206.

Heraclitus. See "Heracleitus of Ephesus" in Freeman, Kathleen, *Ancilla to the Pre-Socratic Philosophers*, pp. 24–34.

Herodotus. *The Histories*. Translated by Aubrey de Selincourt. (Penguin Classics.) Harmondsworth, 1953.

Herzog, Edgar. *Psyche and Death*. Translated by David Cox and Eugene Rolfe. New York: Putnam's Sons for C. G. Jung Foundation, 1966.

Herzog, R. See Aichlin, H.

Hierocles of Alexandria. *Commentary on the Golden Verses (Carmina Aurea) of Pythagoras*. In: F. W. Mullach, *Fragmenta philosophorum Graecorum*. 1860.

Hofmann, Rolf. *Die wichtigsten Körpergottheiten im Huang t'ung chin*. Göppingen: Göppiger Akademiker Beiträge, 1971.

Hoghelande, Theobald de. "De alchemiae difficultatibus." In: *Theatrum chemicum*, Vol. 1, pp. 109–91. Strasburg, 1659.

Horace. *Satires, Epistles, and Ars Poetica*. With an English translation by H. Rushton Fairclough. (Loeb Classical Library.) London/New York: 1929.

Hornung, Erik, ed. *Aegyptische Unterweltsbücher*. Zurich/Munich: Artemis, 1972.

————. *Das Totenbuch der Aegypter*. Zurich/Munich: Artemis, 1979.

Hudson, W. H. *Green Mansions*. In: *Collected Works of W. H. Hudson*, Vol. 12. New York: Dutton, 1923.

*I Ching, or the Book of Changes*. The German translation by Richard Wilhelm, rendered into English by Cary F. Baynes. 2 vols. (Bollingen Series XIX.) New York: Pantheon Books, 1950.

Jacobsohn, Helmut. "The Dialogue of a World-Weary Man with His Ba."

Translated by A. R. Pope. In: Jacobsohn, Helmut, von Franz, Marie-Louise and Hurwitz, Siegmund. *Timeless Documents of the Soul.* Evanston (Ill.): Northwestern University Press, 1968.

———. "Das göttliche Wort und der göttliche Stein." In: *Eranos Jahrbuch,* Vol. 39, 1973.

———, von Franz, Marie-Louise; Hurwitz, Siegmund. *Timeless Documents of the Soul.* Evanston (Ill.): Northwestern University Press, 1968.

Jaffé, Aniela. *Apparitions and Precognition: A Study from the Point of View of C. G. Jung's Analytical Psychology.* Translated by Vera Klein Williams and Mary Eliot. New Hyde Park (New York): University Books, 1963.

———. "Der Tod in der Sicht von C. G. Jung." In: Von Franz, Marie-Louise; Frey-Rohn, Liliane; Jaffé, Aniela. *Im Umkreis des Todes, pp. 11–27.*

Jung, C. G. *Alchemical Studies. Collected Works,* Vol. 13. Translated by R. F. C. Hull. Princeton: Princeton University Press, 1967.

———. *The Archetypes and the Collective Unconscious. Collected Works,* Vol. 9 (1). Translated by R. F. C. Hull. Princeton: Princeton University Press, 1959.

———. *Collected Works of C. G. Jung.* Translated by R. F. C. Hull. (Bollingen Series XX.) 20 vols. Princeton: Princeton University Press, 1953–1978.

———. *Letters,* Vol 1: 1906–1950. Translations from the German by R. F. C. Hull. Princeton: Princeton University Press, 1973.

———. *Letters,* Vol. 2: 1951–1961. Translations from the German by R. F. C. Hull. Princeton: Princeton University Press, 1975.

———. *Memories, Dreams, Reflections.* Recorded and edited by Aniela Jaffé. Translated by R. and C. Winston. New York: Pantheon Books, 1961.

———. *Mysterium Coniunctionis: An Inquiry into the Separation and Synthesis of Psychic Opposites in Alchemy. Collected Works,* Vol. 14. Translated by R. F. C. Hull. Princeton: Princeton University Press, 1963.

———. *Psychology and Alchemy. Collected Works,* Vol. 12. Translated by R. F. C. Hull. Princeton: Princeton University Press, 1953.

———. *Psychology and Religion: West and East. Collected Works,* Vol. 11. Translated by R. F. C. Hull. Princeton: Princeton University Press, 1958.

———. *The Structure and Dynamics of the Psyche. Collected Works,* Vol. 8. Translated by R. F. C. Hull. Princeton: Princeton University Press, 1960.

———; Wilhelm, Richard. *The Secret of the Golden Flower: A Chinese Book of Life.* New York: Harcourt, Brace & World, 1931.

Junker, N. *Die Stundenwachen in den Osirismysterien.* Akademie der Wissenschaft, Vol. 4. Vienna: 1910.

Kees, Hermann. *Totenglauben und Jenseitsvorstellungen der alten Aegypter.* Berlin: Akademie Verlag, 1977.

Kennedy, Emmanuel Xipolitas. *Archetypische Erfahrungen in der Nähe des Todes. Ein Vergleich zwischen "Toderserlebnissen" und "Todesträumen."* Dissertation, University of Innsbruck, 1980. Unpublished.

Kerenyi, Karl. *Hermes der Seelenführer.* Zurich/Munich: Artemis, 1944.

Kübler-Ross, Elisabeth. *Death, the Final Stage of Growth.* Englewood Cliffs (New Jersey): Prentice Hall, 1975.

———. *Living with Death and Dying.* New York: Macmillan, 1981.

———. *On Death and Dying.* New York: Macmillan, 1969.

Kucher, W. *Jenseitsvorstellungen bei den verschiedenen Völkern. Imago Mundi,* Vol. 7. Innsbruck: 1980.

Lampedusa, Guiseppe Di. *The Leopard.* New York: Pantheon Books, 1980.

Lauf, Detlef Ingo. "Im Zeichen des grossen Uebergangs." In: *Leben und Tod in den Religionen,* pp. 8off.

――――. "Nachtodzustand und Wiedergeburt in den Tradition des tibetischen Totenbüchs." In: *Leben nach dem Sterben.*

*Leben nach dem Sterben.* Edited by A. Rosenberg. Munich: Kösel Verlag, 1974.

*Leben und Tod in den Religionen.* Edited by G. Stephenson. Darmstadt: Wissenschaftliche Buchgesellschaft, 1980.

Lechner-Knecht, Sigrid. "Totenbräuche und Jenseitsvorstellungen bei den heutigen Indianern und bei asiatischen Völkern." *Imago Mundi,* Vol. 7. Innsbruck: 1980.

Le Goff, Jacques. *The Birth of Purgatory.* Chicago: Chicago University Press, 1984.

*Lehrbuch der Völkerkunde.* Edited by Hermann Trimborn. Stuttgart: 1958.

Leisegang, H. *Die Gnosis.* Leipzig: Kröner, 1924.

*Lexikon der Suidas.* Berlin: 1854.

Lindley, J. "Near Death Experiences," *Anabiosis, the Journal for Near Death Studies,* No. 1 (December 1981).

Lindsay, Jack. *The Origins of Alchemy in Graeco-Roman Egypt.* London: Frederick Muller, 1970.

Lockhart, Russel A. "Cancer in Myth and Dream: An Exploration into the Relation between Dreams and Disease, "*Spring* 1970, pp. 1–26.

Lopatin, Ivan A. *The Cult of the Dead among the Natives of the Amur Basin.* The Hague: Mouton, 1960.

Lu K'uan Yü. *Taoist Yoga: Alchemy and Immortality.* New York: Wieser, 1970.

Lückel, Kurt. *Begegnung mit Sterbenden.* Munich/Mainz: Kaiser Grünewald, 1981.

Mann, Thomas. *Death in Venice.* Translated by Kenneth Burke. New York: Alfred A. Knopf, 1925.

Mannhardt, W. *Wald- und Feldkulte.* 2 vols. Darmstadt: Wissenschaftliche Buchgesellschaft, 1963.

*Die Märchen der Weltliteratur.* See Aichele, W.

Mattiesen, Emil. *Das persönliche Ueberleben des Todes.* 3 vols. Berlin: W. de Gruyter, 1968.

Mead. G. R. S. *The Doctrine of the Subtle Body in Western Tradition: An Outline of What the Philosophers Thought and Christians Taught on the Subject.* London: Stuart & Watkins, 1967.

Meves, Christa. "Jenseits des Todes." In: *Leben nach dem Sterben,* pp. 70–78.

Meyer, Joachim E. *Tod und Neurose.* Göttingen: Vanderhoeck & Ruprecht, 1973.

Mindell, Arnold. *Dreambody: The Body's Role in Revealing the Self.* Santa Monica (Cal.): Sigo Press, 1982.

Miyuki, Mokusen. *Kreisen des Lichtes: Die Erfahrung der goldenen Blüte.* Weilheim: O. W. Barth, 1972.

Moody, Raymond A. *Life after Life: The Investigation of a Phenomenon—Survival of Bodily Death*. New York: Bantam Books, 1976.

————. *Reflections on Life after Life*. New York: Bantam Books, 1978.

Mookerjee, Ajit. *Tantra Asana: Ein Weg zur Selbstverwirklichung*. Vienna: Schroll, 1971.

Moret, A. *Mystères Egyptiens*. Paris: Colin, 1922.

Neumann, Wolfgang. *Der Mensch und sein Doppelgänger*. Wiesbaden: Steiner, 1981.

Ninck, Martin. *Die Bedeutung des Wassers im Kult und Leben der Alten*. Darmstadt: Wissenschaftliche Buchgesellschaft, 1960.

Nötscher, Friedrich. *Altorientalicher und alttestamentlicher Auferstehungsglaube*. Darmstadt: Wissenschaftliche Buchgesellschaft, 1980.

Olympiodorus. See Berthelot, *Collection des anciens alchimistes grecs*.

Origen. See Mead, G. R. S., *The Doctrine of the Subtle Body in Western Tradition*.

Osis, Karlis; Haraldson, Erlendur. *At the Hour of Death*. New York: Avon, 1980.

Paracelsus. *The Hermetical and Alchemical Writings of Aureolus Philippus Theophrastus Bombast of Hohenheim, called Paracelsus the Great*. Translated by A. E. Waite. London: 1894. 2 vols.

Paulson, J. "Seelungenvorstellungen und Totenglauben bei nordischen Völkern," *Ethos* (Stockholm), Vol. 1/2 (1960).

Pelgrin, Mark. *And a Time to Die*. London: Routledge & Kegan Paul, 1961.

Penfield, Wilder, et al. *The Mystery of the Mind: A Critical Study of Consciousness and the Human Brain*. Princeton: Princeton University Press, 1975.

Philoponus, Johannes. *Philoponi in Aristotelis de Anima*. Edited by M. Hayduck. Berlin: 1897.

Plutarch. *De genio Socratis*. In: *Moralia*. Edited by C. Hubert, et al. Leipzig: 1892–1935. 7 vols. (Vol. 3, pp. 460–511.) English translation by Philemon Holland, revised by C. W. King and A. R. Shilleto; Classical Library, London: 1882–1888.

————. *De sera numinis vindicta*. In: *Moralia*. See Plutarch, *De genio Socratis*.

Pohlhammer, H. G. See Aichlin, H.

Porphyry. *Sententiae ad intelligibilia descendentes*. Edited by Mommert. Leipzig: 1907.

Priestley, J. B. *Man and Time*. London: Aldus, 1969.

Proclus. *Commentaries on the Timaeus of Plato*. Translated by Thomas Taylor. 2 vols. London: 1820.

*Psychotherapeutische Probleme*. Zurich/Stuttgart: Rascher, 1964.

Radford, John. "An Image of Death in Dreams and Ballads," *International Journal of Symbology*, Vol. 6, No. 3 (1975).

Rahim (Iman 'Abd ar-Rahim ibn Ahmad al-Qadi). *Das Totenbuch des Islams*. Munich: Scherz, 1981.

Rahner, Karl. *Zur Theologie des Todes*. Freiburg/Basel/Vienna: Herder, 1961.

Ranke, R. *Indogermanische totenverehrung*, Vol. 1, Folklore Fellow Communications, Vol. LIX, No. 140, pp. 164ff. Helsinki: 1951.

Reeves, Hubert. *Patience dans l'Azur. L'Evolution cosmique*. Paris: Seuil, 1981.

Resch, Andreas, ed. *Fortleben nach dem Tode. Imago Mundi*, No. 7. Innsbruck: Resch Verlag, 1980.

Roeder, Günther. *Urkunden zur Religion des alten Aegypten.* Jena: Diederichs, 1923.

Rosenberg, Alfons, ed. *Leben nach dem Sterben.* Munich: Kösel, 1974.

Sabom, Michael B. *Recollections of Death: A Medical Investigation.* New York: Harper & Row, 1982.

Samburski, S. *Das physikalische Weltbild der Antike.* Zurich/Munich: Artemis, 1965.

Sanford, John A. *Dreams: God's Forgotten Language.* Philadelphia/New York: Lippincott, 1968.

Sborowitz, A. (ed.). *Der leidende Mensch.* Darmstadt: Wissenschaftliche Buchgesellschaft, 1960.

Schopenhauer, Arthur. *Parerga und Paralipomena.* Zurich: Diogenes, 1977.

Sixtus of Siena. *Biblioteca Sancta Venetiis.* Venice: 1566.

Sprocktoff, J. F. "Der feindliche Tote." In: *Leben und Tod in den Religionen.*

Steffen, Uwe. *Das Mysterium von Tod und Auferstehung.* Göttingen: Vanderhoeck & Ruprecht, 1963.

Stephenson, Gunther, ed. *Leben und Tod in den Religionen: Symbol und Wirklichkeit.* Darmstadt: Wissenschaftliche Buchgesellschaft, 1980.

Steuer, Robert. *Ueber das wohlriechende Natron bei den alten Aegypter.* Leiden: Brill, 1937.

Sundermeier, Theo. "Todesriten und Lebenssymbole in den afrikanischen Religionen." In: *Leben und Tod in den Religionen.*

Tertullian. *De carnis resurrectione. Corpus scriptorum Latinorum Academiae Vindobonensis*, Vol. 47 (1906). English translation by C. Dodgson, In: *Library of the Fathers*, Vol. 10. Oxford: 1842.

Thausing, Gertrud. "Altägyptisches religiöses Gedankengut im heutigen Afrika." In: *Leben und Tod in den Religionen.*

———. *Der Auferstehungsgedanke in ägyptischen religiösen Texten.* Leipzig: Kroner, 1943.

*Totenbuch der Aegypter.* See Hornung, E.

Trimborn, Hermann (ed.). *Lehrbuch der Völkerkunde.* Stuttgart: 1958.

Uhde, Bernard. "Psyche ein Symbol?" In: *Leben und Tod in den Religionen.*

Vermeule, Emily. *Aspects of Death in Early Greek Art and Poetry.* Berkeley: University of California Press, 1979.

Vorbichler, A. "Das Leben in Rhythmus von Tod und Wiedergeburt in der Vorstellung der schwarzafrikanischen Völker." In: *Leben und Tod in den Religionen.*

Wheelwright, Jane. *The Death of a Woman.* New York: St. Martin's Press, 1981.

Whitmont, Edward C. *The Symbolic Quest.* New York: G. P. Putnam's Sons, 1969.

Widengren, Georg. *Mani und der Manichaeismus.* Stuttgart: Kohlhammer, 1961.

Wiesner Joseph. *Grab und Jenseits: Untersuchungen im ägäischen Raum der Bronzezeit und Eisenzeit.* Berlin: Töpelmann, 1938.

Wilhelm, Richard. *Weisheit des Ostens.* Düsseldorf/Cologne: Diederichs, 1951.

———— and Jung, C. G. *The Secret of the Golden Flower: A Chinese Book of Life.* New York: Harcourt, Brace & World, 1931.

Wit, Constant de. *Le rôle et le sens du lion dans l'Egypte ancienne.* Leiden: Brill, 1951.

*Zigeuner Märchen.* See Aichele, W.

Zosimos of Panopolis. See Berthelot, *Collection des anciens alchimistes grecs*, Vol. 2, "Les Oeuvres de Zosime," pp. 107–252.

# Index